Young, Restless, No Longer Reformed

Young, Restless, No Longer Reformed

Black Holes, Love, and a
Journey In and Out of Calvinism

AUSTIN FISCHER

CASCADE *Books* · Eugene, Oregon

Cascade Books
An Imprint of Wipf and Stock Publishers
199 W. 8th Ave., Suite 3
Eugene, OR 97401

www.wipfandstock.com

ISBN 13: 978-1-62564-151-9

Cataloging-in-Publication data:

Fischer, Austin.

    Young, restless, no longer Reformed : black holes, love, and a journey in and out of Calvinism / Austin Fischer.

    xiv + 116 p.; 23 cm—Includes bibliographical references.

    ISBN 13: 978-1-62564-151-9

    1. Arminianism. 2. Calvinism. I. Title.

BT751.3 F56 2014

Manufactured in the USA.

To Allison—
A constant reminder that discussions are nice but love is the real deal.

Contents

Foreword

If I were a Calvinist, I would not only want to read this book—I'd want to read it with my Calvinist friends. Not only is it too good to read alone—I'd want to parse our way through it, pondering each point Austin Fischer makes. After all, he was one of the resurgent Calvinists. Plus, he's got a bundle of wonderful expressions.

What do we call this new wave of Calvinists? At one time I called them the "NeoReformed" but a few (truly) Reformed people informed me this resurgence of Calvinism was not really Reformed. "How," one of them asked, "can someone be Reformed and not believe in infant baptism and utilize the classic Reformed confessions?" Some then called them the "NeoCalvinists" but this term—I was reminded by a professor friend who was a specialist in this area—won't work because that described the Kuyperians. So another scholar set down some firm lines of thinking when he said the resurgent Calvinists are really "NeoPuritans." Then a friend of mine told me this was a slur since, in his mind, "Puritan" was derogatory. But anyone who knows American history—most especially the founding of Massachusetts Bay Company under the likes of John Winthrop—wonders how this resurgent group can be called Puritans. They don't have the kind of power needed to do the things the Puritans did. What did the Puritans do? They tried to establish a Christian nation with Christian cities, even if they were committed to acceptance of those who were unlike them, something time proved to be more than a challenge for those early Puritans.

So what do we call the resurgent Calvinists? Do we need a name or a label? Yes—I think—because humans *cannot not* categorize and label and define, and because good thinking requires discernment, and discernment requires nuance. That is why we need to see resurgent Calvinism as a kind of NeoPuritanism. Most of them are Baptists or Free Church types, though some of the more notable leaders and plenty of their followers are parts of historic Reformed groups.

So who are we talking about? That's fairly obvious: John Piper, who single-handedly (on the generous platform of his friend Louie Giglio) made NeoPuritanism attractive; Tim Keller, whose graceful leadership and single-focused winsome books have offered a full platform of pastoral theology; and D. A. Carson, whose laser-like thinking offers compelling answers along NeoPuritan lines of thinking. Add the numbers one gets with the Southern Baptists whose Calvinism has been reshaped under the leadership of Al Mohler, and we've got a powerful movement underway. With charismatic leadership and intellectual giftedness like this, it is no wonder NeoPuritanism plays so well in the American scene, especially since its free market approach to religion allows individual pastors to mix and match their theology and their church vision into similar lines of thinking.

This is what attracted Austin, and this is what will continue to attract young, theologically hungry evangelicals. There are other options, like Missio Alliance or traditional denominations, but The Gospel Coalition and Together for the Gospel have established their voices as the center for NeoPuritanism, or if you prefer, resurgent Calvinism.

Calvinism, we perhaps need to remind ourselves, is not new. Nor are its problems recent discoveries. Austin Fischer both listened to these recent voices and learned to think his way through them . . . and has found the whole sound wanting. One way he has framed it is in these words: "But I believe we best say *yes* to God's glory and sovereignty by saying *no* to Calvinism." Those in the camp know these words cut to the heart of NeoPuritanism's theological vision.

I had Austin's experience. As a college student, I fell in love with the architecture of Calvinism. I read a sermon from Spurgeon each day for months and months, I read John Owen bit by bit, and John Brown on Hebrews, and I drank in the wine of Calvinism until I was inebriated in the best sense of the word. I loved it—I loved its fine lines of thinking, and I think what I liked most is that it both put me in my place and God in his, and I liked that sense of all things being where they ought to be. Until I encountered passages in the Bible that shook that theology to the core.

I had been star-struck by Calvinist theologians and still was, but I found the exegesis less than compelling. Passage after passage convinced me that while the big picture—God's glory in the face of Christ—was as good as our theology can get, the finer nuances just didn't work with how the Bible frames the freedom of God's love and human responsiveness. For a number of years I wandered between Calvinism and other options, eventually settling for what I sometimes call "Anabaptism with Anglican sensibilities." I still read Calvin and Piper and Edwards, but with a hermeneutic of suspicion. I like their architecture, even if their furnishings need to be tossed into the garbage heap. I like the idea of God's glory, but God's love is the final end—not God's glory.

What I most appreciate about Austin's story is its honesty, its struggle, and its confident, clear voice, shaped by a deep humbling—he thought he had it right, but learned that the Bible tells an even better story, one he has embraced. I like how he puts it: "Faith, doubt, humility, and confidence— this is the stuff and substance of theology at its best. Swagger, smugness, and certainty—this is the stuff and substance of ideology at its worst." Naked encounters with rugged realities awakened a theological humility.

No one, he learned, can look Auschwitz in the face and not wonder how such a colossal act of barbaric evil can square with a God who determines all things. No one, he also learned, can stare at the prospects of hell in the traditional sense and not wonder about the goodness of God—or at least ask "Why?" And why would God create so many—the numbers stagger—knowing that most (again in the traditional Calvinist sense) will be there suffering forever and ever? In other words, he learned he had to believe some really horrible things about God to sustain his Calvinism. As Austin says it, "And this is what happened to me at the core of the black hole of self-glorifying deity: the lights went out and I was left sitting in the dark in an absurd universe with an enigmatic deity of naked power."

And that God, he concluded, was not the God of the Bible. This book tells his story, and I hope you read it, and I hope you get a bunch of friends to read it together. Talk about it and ask one question, "Which view of God is best?" Or, "Is the Calvinist God the God of the Bible?" Or better yet, "Is the Calvinist God the God we discover when we look into the face of Jesus, the incarnation of God?" Austin tells his answers to these questions at the age many need to begin answering these questions.

Scot McKnight
Professor of New Testament
Northern Seminary

Acknowledgements

Many people have had a hand in forming me and thus in forming this book—too many hands to count. But here are a few...

Allison, Dad, Mom, Adam, Marilyn, Mikey, Da, and Pop—who wants a perfect family when you have a family that loves you?

Belinda, Austin, and Nanny—the family I didn't know I was missing.

Joel—mentor, friend, and theological sparring partner in the healthiest of ways.

Roger Olson—a brilliant teacher but even more generous soul, and we both know this book isn't here without your help.

Nate Hansen—your literary suggestions made this book a lot better.

Friends—sorry you've had to listen to me talk about all this stuff over the years, but thanks for listening and encouraging me, and maybe I'll stop talking about it now.

Introduction

Black Holes

Gravity

When a big star dies, a remarkable thing can happen.[1] Its own gravity crunches it until it becomes a small core of unimaginable density—matter squeezed together so tightly the known laws of physics cease to exist. The dead star now has a gravitational pull so strong that nothing, not even light, can escape. And at this point, the dead star has become a black hole, and everything within its reach is dragged towards its center. It can swallow planets, stars, and even other black holes. Get too close and you've bought a one-way ticket on a journey to the center of a black hole. Its gravity is irresistible.

Gravity is an integral part of human life. It doesn't take us long to learn that what comes up must come down. And it's not as if anyone enforces gravity—it just *is*; a physical force to be accepted and not conquered. Gravity is also a spiritual force in the sense that we humans find ourselves drawn to things beyond our control. We are constantly sucked in to things—a job, a person, a hobby, an addiction. But of course if you really put spiritual gravity under the microscope, you see that the thing we are being sucked in to is ourselves.

We are black holes—walking, talking pits of narcissism, self-pity, and loneliness, pillaging the world around us in a desperate attempt to fill the void inside us. Unless something is done, you will spend the rest of your existence as a human black hole, eternally collapsing in on self in a tragic effort to preserve self. It's bad news.

But Christians believe there is good news that is better than the bad news. We believe something has been done—that through the incarnation, crucifixion, and resurrection of Jesus Christ, God has done what we could not do ourselves. We no longer have to live under the crushing gravity of self because where sin and selfishness abounded, grace now abounds all the more. It certainly is good news, but…

Options for the Restless

Leave it to us to take something so beautiful and other-centered and turn it into something (you guessed it) about us.

The universe-altering message of the gospel becomes a message about me: Jesus died so I can be happy and comfortable forever and ever. While this may pass for gospel in many circles, there is a growing swell of opposition to it in many others—a recognition that such thin, therapeutic, self-centered expressions of Christianity lack the gravitas to hold a human life together, much less make it thrive. A crowd of voices calls us out of consumerism, moralism, and skepticism and into sacrifice, risk, and commitment.

And for those who are restless for more, Neo-Calvinism[2] often appears as the strongest—and perhaps only—alternative for thinking biblical people. It offers the new center of gravity that can finally draw us away from self. Such was my conviction, and I still believe Neo-Calvinism is a strong alternative to cultural Christianity.

But I believe we best say *yes* to God's glory and sovereignty by saying *no* to Calvinism. I believe that I—along with many others, past and present—have found an even better option. It's not new, and it's not novel; indeed I would argue it is simply the historic consensus of the church. But correctly understood, it offers the greatest hope for a restless church. Unlike Calvinism, it doesn't replace the black hole of self with the black hole of deity, making both God and the Bible impossible (more on that later); however, it does offer an infinitely glorious God, a crucified Messiah, and a cross-shaped call to follow Jesus.

Egotistical Sincerity

These are my convictions, and anyone with convictions faces a dilemma: would you rather be convincing or honest? Is it more important to get people to agree with you or to honestly present the best of worthy options?

While I have certainly tried to be convincing, I think the truth is best served when we are honest, and so I have also tried to be honest. And the best way I have found to be honest is to tell you my story: a journey in and out of Calvinism. As Chesterton once confessed, sometimes you have to be egotistical if you want to be sincere.[3]

In this reminiscing, something became clear: theology and biography belong together.[4] We try to make sense of God as we try to make sense of our own stories, our own lives. As such, theology is meant for participants, not spectators. I write as a participant and not a spectator in the hope it will help you become a better participant in your own theological journey, wherever it takes you. These things said, let the journey begin. Only it can't quite begin without two quick detours.

Detour #1: The Wrong Girl

I once had a friend who was convinced the wrong girl was the right girl. He thought she hung the moon while walking on water and while I thought she was nice and all, I was convinced there was someone out there better for him. Whether I was right or wrong isn't the point—the point is that when I talked with him about it, I wasn't trying to sabotage his current relationship so much as I was trying to encourage the prospects of a new one. I feel much the same when I talk to people about Calvinism, because while I think you could put a ring on her and live happily ever after, I also think there's someone better out there. On top of that, it's a shame to be known for what you're against, so for clarity's sake, I'm not trying to get anyone to *not be* something (a Calvinist), but *to be* something.

Or to make the point with different strokes, the silhouette of the crucified God of Golgotha is an image chiseled into my heart. When sin within rises, chaos without descends, confusion all around lays waste to any semblance of comprehension—when I don't feel like I understand a damn thing—I look up there and I understand enough to say *thank you*. I understand enough to call it *love*. And I watch as it casts sparks of light into previously darkened corners.

So when someone messes with this picture, adding a cryptic backdrop that threatens to stain the whole thing, I'm against the backdrop only because I'm for the picture I think the backdrop ruins. I'm not against the Calvinist picture of God so much as I am grieved by what that picture does to the picture I love, turning the full-truth of Golgotha into a duplicitous half-truth. The rest of this book is a description of what happened when my Calvinism was subjected to the searing scrutiny of that image, in the hopes you might glimpse the terrifyingly beautiful God of Jesus Christ.

Detour #2: Everything

The most devastating combination of words in the English language form a statement masquerading as a question: who cares? When this "question" is asked, a statement is made. The asker is expressing his apathy and disregard for the issue under discussion. It does not appear to matter, so why waste our breath? Why kick a hornet's nest just so we can count the hornets? And it's a good "question" to ask because many of the issues that hoard our energies and efforts are dead ends. It's also a "question" I've been asked many times when debates about Calvinism and its alternatives arise.

Does it really matter if Calvinism is true or false? Does it really matter if we have free will? Does it really matter? Not at all, and yet, more than you could imagine.

No, it doesn't matter because God is who he is and does what he does regardless of what we think of him, in much the same sense that the solar system keeping spinning around the sun even if we're convinced it spins around the earth. Our opinions about God will not change God; *however, they can most certainly change us.* And so yes, it does matter because the conversations about Calvinism and free will plunge into the heart of the question the universe asks us at every turn:

Who is God?

And this is a question that has everything to do with everything.

Endnotes

1. For a good explanation of how black holes are formed, see Stephen Hawking, *Black Holes and Baby Universes and Other Essays* (New York: Bantam, 1993), 103–4.

2. Neo-Calvinism proper is a Dutch strand of Calvinism associated with Abraham Kuyper. I am using it to refer to the high federal Calvinism of Jonathan Edwards, as popularized by people like John Piper, Mark Driscoll, Al Mohler, etc. The term was used in this fashion in a *Time* magazine article (March 12, 2009) and seems to have stuck. As such, I am using it to delineate the New Calvinism movement chronicled in Collin Hansen's *Young, Restless, and Reformed* (Wheaton, IL: Crossway, 2008), although I acknowledge some people prefer to call it other things (for example, Neo-Puritanism).

3. G. K. Chesterton, *Orthodoxy* (N.P.: Simon & Brown, 2012), 3.

4. This idea is explored in *Biography as Theology*, by James McClendon (Eugene, OR: Wipf and Stock, 2002).

1

A Blind Date with Calvinism

Why No One Starts Out a Calvinist

You have free will and you know it. You can order sweet tea or Coke, you can hit sand wedge or driver, you can open this book or close it. Like I said, you're free and you know it . . . only you don't know it.

When it comes down to it, you can never know whether you really have free will (just try to prove it to yourself). Maybe you couldn't have ordered a Coke, hit the driver, or closed the book. Maybe it's all determined. Maybe everything—love and hate, birth and death, joys and sorrows, sinners and saints, heaven and hell—unfolds according to some predetermined, eternal blueprint in the mind of God. There's no way to know for sure.

But we certainly experience ourselves as free if nothing else, which is why no one starts out a Calvinist. It just doesn't seem to make much sense at first glance, and for many this is enough to dismiss Calvinism and never bother giving it a second look. And yet those with the courage to gaze a bit deeper quickly discover it will not be tossed aside so easily. It has a magnetism, a defiant pull. Its gravity is irresistible.

Young and Restless

I was introduced to Calvinism on a blind date with John Piper—I should probably explain.

I was in high school and had the "more" itch, and if you're reading this book you probably know the one I'm talking about. I wanted more out of faith, more out of life, more out of God and had the sense God wanted more out of me. I was young and restless, so my youth pastor recommended I read *Desiring God*, by John Piper, and offered to discuss it with me.

I walked away with more questions than epiphanies, but what I did understand struck a chord: he was scratching the "more" itch. God doesn't care whether or not I have the American Dream, upward mobility, a cushy vacation home in the Hamptons, or a fat pension to lounge on when I retire. And while we're at it, God isn't my personal self-esteem coach whose only goal in life is to put powder on my bottom and tell me how special I am. My comfort and self-esteem are not God's priorities. God cares about God and wants me to care about God.

All of this is summed up by a short phrase that is the animating impulse of Neo-Calvinism[1]: *It's all about God's glory.* All as in *everything.* As the adage goes, "The chief end of God is to glorify God and enjoy displaying and magnifying his glory forever."[2] And if we don't like it, if we think that sounds egotistical or self-centered, then we would do well to remember that when you're God, it's OK for you to be a narcissistic black hole. In fact, it's not only OK, but it's good and gracious because what humans need most is more God, not more self-esteem or navel-gazing. Thus, Piper asks the pointed question: "Do you feel most loved by God because he makes much of you, or because he frees you to enjoy making much of him forever?"[3] That stings a little, but in a good way, and it gets better.

Piper also teaches "Christian hedonism." Humans were made for pleasure and what brings us supreme pleasure is the worship and adoration of the one thing in all existence of infinite value: God. In other words, God's self-exaltation and our joy are not opposing pursuits but dovetail together in perfect symmetry: God is most glorified in us when we are most satisfied in him.[4] Living a life for the glory of God is the most joyful, exciting, and compelling thing you can do with the fleeting existence you're given on earth.

And did I mention that the Bible talks about God's self-glorification a lot?[5]

God Dies

So when I reached the end of my blind date with Calvinism, everything I knew had been called into question—my faith, my theology, my way of life. And while I had hated it, I had loved it.

Anyone who has been through theological deconstruction knows the feeling. Your deepest and most cherished (or perhaps most assumed) views of God and self have been poked and prodded and as you desperately seek to plug all the holes there is the nagging sense that maybe this view just needs to die. Maybe this god needs six feet of dirt shoveled over him so that something closer to the real God can come walking out of the tomb.

I knew my god needed to die. I knew I was awash in Christianity that had little to do with Jesus and a lot to do with me—my comfort, my security, my stuff, my appeased conscience, my mansion in heaven. I knew I needed a new God and was confident John Piper was introducing me to him. But I also knew there were a few bullets that needed biting before I could sign off on the dotted line of Calvinism.

Biting Bullets and Counting Sheep

"So you're telling me . . . "

If you've ever tried to explain Calvinism to someone for the first time, this will be the first phrase out of her mouth. It speaks to the initial shock and skepticism people feel when it is suggested that God is the all-determining reality: that is, that every single thing that happens has been rendered certain (ordained) by God because there is nothing God does not either directly or indirectly cause. It is a bedrock belief of Calvinism, but comes with some obvious baggage.

"So you're telling me that God has already determined everyone who will be in heaven and hell?" This big, ugly question is what anyone who wrestles with Calvinism must square off with sooner or later, and it was a tough question for me to get a handle on. How was that fair? How was it fair for God to choose to save some and then send everyone else to hell? I should have seen the answer coming: you don't want fair. Fair would mean we all get what we deserve and what we all deserve is hell. Fair = hell. Well that's fair enough, I suppose.

But of course the rabbit hole goes a bit deeper than that. Because maybe we don't want fair so much as we want love. In other words, perhaps our problem with the idea that God has unconditionally predetermined who to save and who to condemn is that it doesn't seem loving, and the Bible certainly tells us God is loving.[6] Furthermore, if God has determined everything, hasn't God also determined the sins that he is going to send people to hell forever for? Hasn't God made sure that people will commit the sins he will then judge them for? If so, how is that just? And then there's the question that pulls together these issues of love and justice: how is God good? If—before the creation of a single human being—God chose to send people to hell for sins he ordained they would commit, how is he good? If that question doesn't make you count out a crowded flock of sheep on a sleepless night, I'm not sure what will.

Mystery and Transcendence

In searching for answers, I became acquainted with two terms that became a staple of my theological thought and vocabulary: mystery and transcendence. You know the verse: "'For My thoughts are not your thoughts, nor are your ways My ways,' declares the Lord. 'For as the heavens are higher than the earth, so are My ways higher than your ways and My thoughts than your thoughts.'"[7]

The problem with theology is that it's humans doing it. Finite, fragile, fallen creatures are trying to make sense of their Creator. Mistakes and hilarity are bound to ensue. As Frederick Buechner says, "Theology is the study of God and his ways. For all we know, dung beetles may study us and our ways and call it humanology. If so, we would probably be more touched and amused than irritated. One hopes that God feels likewise."[8]

All of this to say, God is above and beyond us. In theological terms, God is transcendent. God is not just Superman minus the cape and red underwear—a being like us only way stronger and nicer. No, God exists on a completely different plane, shrouded in the veil of divine mystery. God is *not* like us. And this means that we cannot simply project onto God all the virtues we find desirable as humans. We cannot assume that God's love, justice, and goodness match up perfectly with our notions of love, justice, and goodness. To do so is to make a "category mistake," to treat God like a super-creature instead of the Creator. We might find it difficult to understand how it's just for God to send people to hell for sins he ordained they commit, but who are we to question God's justice? Who are we to put God in a box, telling him what he can and cannot do, who he can and cannot be? Or as Paul says, "Who are you, O man, to answer back to God?"[9]

Bottom

When you come to bottom of the rabbit hole, this is the mystery waiting for you. How is God loving, just, or good when he sends people to hell for sins he ordained they commit? While there are countless attempts to explain this dilemma, the most responsible answers eventually capitulate to the mystery. We cannot know exactly how God is loving, just, or good in light of his electing some and not electing others. But we can know that God is completely sovereign over his creation, is the all-determining reality, holds us accountable for our sins, and does everything for his own glory.[10]

And this is what it all comes down to: are you willing to live with this mystery?

Will you accept the idea that you and I and everyone who has ever lived will be sent to eternal bliss or damnation based on an inscrutable, unconditional decision of God? Will you affirm that God will send people to hell for sins he made certain they would commit? Will you worship a God who might have created you in order to damn you?

Like many others who have traveled this road, I struggled and complained and went kicking and screaming, but eventually I bit the bullet and did so for the same reason that most every thoughtful Calvinist I know has: I didn't feel as though the Bible left me any option.

The Bible Tells Me So

As a Christian—and a Protestant evangelical at that—I care about the Bible. If the Bible teaches it, I want to believe it because I believe God speaks through scripture. And while the "battle for the Bible" is a complex and nuanced issue with those on the left accusing those on the right of bibliolatry (treating the Bible as a fourth member of the Trinity) and those on the right accusing those on the left of undermining biblical authority,

I would think we could agree that if the Bible teaches it, we should try to believe it.[11]

I had become convinced the Bible taught Calvinism so I surrendered and dove in. John Piper speaks of a similar dive in a candid and poignant remembrance of his conversion to Calvinism:

> So when I went to college and began to hear people give a framework to this [Calvinism], I revolted against the sovereignty of God . . . When I arrived at Fuller Seminary, I took a class on systematic theology with James Morgan . . . and another with Dan Fuller on hermeneutics. And coming from both sides—theology and exegesis—I was feeling myself absolutely cornered by all the evidences of God's sovereignty in the Bible . . . I would put my face in my hands in my room, and I would just cry because my world was coming apart. I just couldn't figure anything out . . . But at the end of James Morgan's theology class, I wrote in a blue book: "Romans 9 is like a tiger going around devouring free-willers like me." And it did.[12]

Romans 9 *is* like a tiger going around devouring free-willers. If you have read Romans 9 and don't find it the least bit possible it's affirming unconditional election and predestination—as well as defending God's justice in both—then you're kidding yourself. And for me, it wasn't just possible—it was probable, maybe even certain. I was young, restless, and now I was Reformed.[13]

2

Roots of Certainty, Seeds of Doubt

Sagittarius A*

At the center of the Milky Way galaxy, there is a frenzy of energy and motion. Imploding stars, searing solar winds, swirling gases—a cosmic whirlpool of light and heat. And yet at the very center of the center of our galaxy, in a region called Sagittarius A*, the lights go out. A dark entity resides there. Immune to the surrounding chaos, it spins these stars, winds, and gases round and round. At the very center of the center of the galaxy, there is a supermassive black hole, maintaining galactic order as it tries to yank billions of stars and planets into its core.[14]

Once I bit the bullet and said *yes* to Calvinism, it brought my previously chaotic faith into order. God's glory was Sagittarius A* and everything else fell into place around it. But what exactly does this mean? What do we mean when we say, "It's all about God's glory"? And what happens to everything else when everything is about God's glory? Curiosity got the best of me, and I found myself inching closer and closer to a supermassive black hole.

God Wants Everyone to Be Saved . . . ?

God wants everyone to be saved.[15] Let that sink in a bit.

Hitler, Osama bin Laden, your mother-in-law.[16] God wants everyone to be saved, and there's really not much argument about it. But not everyone is going to be saved.[17] Despite some very thoughtful arguments to the contrary,[18] scripture just won't let us affirm universalism. In other words, while God most certainly has the right to save everyone, he has not given us much of a right to believe everyone will be saved. Let that sink in a bit: God wants everyone to be saved, but not everyone is going to be saved. In some sense, God is not going to get what God wants.

We are used to not getting what we want. Not getting what you want is part of being human. But how can God want something and not get it? Well, God must want something else more than he wants everyone to be saved. And again, there's really not much argument about it. The argument surfaces when we attempt to explain what God wants more than the salvation of everyone. There are really only two answers.

For free-will theism, the answer is loving, reciprocal relationship. In other words, God chooses not to save all because that would undermine our ability to freely accept and reciprocate God's love. So if God were to "force" us into salvation, it would make our existence utterly redundant, for if God wanted to be eternally surrounded by creatures incapable of genuine relationality, one supposes he would have stopped creating on the fifth day.

But what answer could Calvinism offer? If freely accepted and reciprocated love does not matter to God and God wants everyone to be saved, why doesn't God save everyone? To answer this, we have to talk about why God created the world.

Glory, Glory, Glory

People with regal, white, powdered wigs look like they mean business, and in the case of Jonathan Edwards, looks are not deceiving. He was a brilliant theologian, preeminent expositor of Calvinism, and was pretty confident he knew why God created the world:

Glory.

God created the world for his glory, or more precisely, for his self-glorification. Edwards explains what this means:

Thus it appears reasonable to suppose, that it was God's last end, that there might be a glorious and abundant emanation of his infinite fullness . . . and that the disposition to communicate himself, or diffuse his own fullness, was what moved him to create the world.[19]

The glory of God is the manifold greatness and goodness of who God is. Love, justice, mercy, wrath, power, compassion—bundle them together and you get glory. But without a creation, some of these things would never find expression. How could God show his mercy or justice if all that existed was God? The Son showing mercy to the Spirit for . . . being perfect?

So God creates to flex his glory muscles, to allow the full manifestation of all he is; that is to say, the ultimate end for which God created the world was to display the full range of his glory. So why doesn't God save everyone? Because while God wants to save everyone, what God wants even more is to display the fullness of his glory. As such, God ordains the eternal damnation of the humans he also wants to save because he wants to display his wrath and justice even more than he wants to save them. When it comes down to it, God values his self-glorification above their salvation. It's all about God's glory—meaning, everything circles around the supermassive black hole of God's desire to show the universe what being God is all about.

Horses in Heaven and Imaging God

I have a friend who thinks there are going to be horses in heaven because she likes horses. I don't know whether or not there are going to be horses in heaven,[20] but I do know that claiming there will be horses because you like horses is pretty thin logic. But in addition to being thin logic, it's also an amusing example of a not-so-amusing problem: human-centered theology.

"You can safely assume you've created God in your own image when it turns out that God hates all the same people you do."[21] As an old pastor I know used to say, "If you can't say amen, might as well say ouch." It's scary how effortlessly and intuitively we create God in our own image. It's also brilliant—if you "create" a "God" who loves everything you love and hates everything you hate and thinks everything you think, then you've got it made. You get to do and be and think whatever you want, and God can't say or do anything about it because you've already decided what God can and cannot say and do.

Of course few, if any, would knowingly do such a thing; rather, we do it subconsciously, instinctively. As little walking black holes, our strongest instinct is self-preservation, and what better way to preserve self than by creating a "God" who will divinely authorize our preservation instincts? This is why—if we squint closely enough—we'll see that most of us have rubbed off on "God" more than God has rubbed off on us.

And this is what human-centered theology does: it creates God in our own image. And as my Reformed roots were growing deeper, I began to suspect it was the culprit behind any and all rejections of Calvinism and its self-glorifying God. As alluded to earlier, if it doesn't seem loving or just for God to eternally punish you for sins he ordained you commit, that's because you are treating God like a human. You're forgetting that God's love, justice, and goodness dwarf your feeble, soft, humanistic understandings of them. You may wish God loved the way you think he should, but your wishing doesn't make it so. You may wish God was most concerned with your glory, but scripture teaches us that he's not.

Two Bills

Bill O'Reilly and Bill Maher are the bane of many people's—and probably each other's—existence. They both host popular political television talk shows: O'Reilly's is conservative; Maher's is liberal. They are also both very persuasive and very obnoxious. Listen to either of them long enough and they will say something you hate, but can't help agreeing with, but still want to fight them over because they have rubbed your nose in it.

Calvinism tends to rub your nose in your humanity. And it's offensive and obnoxious and makes you want to jump in the DeLorean,[22] set the date to 1750, gun it up to 88 mph, and then rip off Jonathan Edwards's powdered wig and give him a piece of your mind. But in the final analysis, Calvinism rubs your nose in your humanity because it believes the Bible rubs your nose in your humanity.

My nose had been rubbed in it, I had accepted it, I no longer wanted to fight Jonathan Edwards, and the painful process of theological deconstruction and reconstruction was complete. I had a new God, a glorious God, the biblical God. I had God.

The Chasm of Transcendence

Only we never *have* God.

And no matter how certain we are that we have God, we certainly cannot be certain that it is indeed God we have. Certainty is not possible when the finite is bumping up against the infinite. It's not possible when a person is trying to know another person. If you want to treat God like God and like a personal God at that, you have to let certainty go.

But doesn't this leave us in the fog of skepticism, floating off into empty space without an anchor? In a word, no. There is a great distance between skepticism and confidence and an equally great distance between confidence and certainty. God helps us bridge the gap between skepticism and confidence, but he doesn't seem particularly concerned with building us a bridge from confidence to certainty. Due to the nature of the divine/human relationship, the gap between confidence and certainty is an unbridgeable chasm. It is the chasm of transcendence and transcendence is an equal opportunity offender: everyone gets their nose rubbed in it.

The chasm of transcendence means there will always be seeds of doubt to undermine our roots of certainty, and that is no fun. But more importantly, it means that God will always have room to surprise us, room to be who he is and not who he is supposed to be. And when God has room to be God, you never know where you might end up.

3

One Hell of a Problem
(The Girl in the Red Jacket)

Searching for Silver Bullets

Humans love silver bullets: quick, clean, indisputable solutions to complex problems. How do we take care of the poor in our country? Elect a Democrat. How do we save more marriages? Make wives respect their husbands. How can we be certain God exists? All humans share moral absolutes. What more needs to be said? Plenty, actually.

Everyone is looking for silver bullets because they make things easy. They dilute complicated issues into trite syllogisms. They get us off the hook, offering us peace without wrestling, security without risk, tranquility without chaos. Christians are especially susceptible to silver-bullet fever. We are like silver-bullet mercenaries, scouring the Bible for their glimmer so we can pluck them out, load them up, and exact the fatal kill shot on all dissenting opinions and beliefs, putting the matter to rest.

But the problem with silver bullets is they do not exist. They are a mirage, an offer of victory too easily won. And when it comes to the debate over Calvinism and free-will theism, there are no silver bullets, be they biblical, theological, or philosophical. If there were, one suspects the debate would have been settled long ago.

Big changes usually have inauspicious beginnings. Something happens, something is said, something takes root and a tiny seed is sown. In this seed are the beginnings of conversion, the slab for a new home, a different trajectory for thinking, doing, and being. But this conversion will only come about slowly, the gradual emergence of a green sprout poking up through rocky ground. I had been a reluctant convert to Calvinism, but was now deeply influenced by its pull. Any move away from it would not come easy.

Theology 1301

Who is God?

How do you know?

From the Christian perspective, these are *the* questions of human existence. All other questions asked and answers given ultimately bend back toward these, for in every answer to every question there is the implicit claim, "This is who God is and this is how I know." And so who is God and how do you know?

I still remember my first real encounter with these questions. I was a precocious freshmen theology major (a volatile combination) and thanks to people like the holy trinity of Johns—Calvin, Edwards, and Piper—I came to college fairly assured I had the answers. God was the self-glorifying, all-determining reality who did everything for his glory, and I knew it because the Bible told me so. Can I have my diploma now?

But one of the best things about college (or simply reading a book!) is that you are forced to converse with people who are, bluntly, smarter than you. They've read more, experienced more, thought more, reflected more, and prayed more. You may nevertheless disagree with them, but you can no longer live under the illusion that their positions are easily dismissed. And during my freshman year of college, one professor in particular was a nagging thorn in my Calvinist side.

Some say the best teachers do not give us the right answers so much as teach us to ask the right questions; for until we are asking the right questions, we surely cannot come to the right answers. And after a year-long match of biblical and theological tennis, my professor finally volleyed over something that landed right at my feet and refused an easy return. But it wasn't as if I had never thought about or seen it before. It was just that now it was ruthlessly exposed so that I could see it for what it was, and I had to admit . . . it was one hell of a problem.

Auschwitz and Evil

It is often said that one's theology is not tenable unless it can be preached at the gates of Auschwitz. So if you couldn't stomach sharing what you believe about God to the Jewish men, women, and children staring down the barrel of extermination at the hands of evil incarnate, then you would do well to pursue some alternatives. All of this to say, the problem posed by evils such as the Holocaust and countless others is a grim darkness surrounding and often mocking our most cherished beliefs about God. God is all good and all powerful and yet evil, horrendous evil, exists. What gives?

To address the problem, both Calvinism and free-will theism employ greater good arguments: that is, God allows (free-will theism) or ordains (Calvinism) evil for some greater good. As alluded to previously, in free-will theism God allows evil because it is an inevitable possibility in a world constituted by free beings. If God is to achieve the apparently great good of loving, reciprocal relationship with his creatures, then evil is something God must allow (more on this later).

Of course in Calvinism, God ordains evil for the full manifestation of his glory. Borrowing again from Jonathan Edwards:

> If it were not right that God should decree and permit and pun-
> ish sin, there could be no manifestation of God's holiness in
> hatred of sin, or in showing any preference, in his providence,
> of godliness before it. There would be no manifestation of God's
> grace or true goodness, if there was no sin to be pardoned, no
> misery to be saved from . . . So evil is necessary, in order to the
> highest happiness of the creature, and the completeness of that
> communication of God, for which he made the world; because
> the creature's happiness consists in the knowledge of God, and
> the sense of his love. And if the knowledge of him be imperfect,
> the happiness of the creature must be proportionally imperfect.[23]

According to Edwards, God ordains evil so he can display his holiness in judging it and his grace in forgiving it, and this is good for us because it allows us to behold the fullness of God's glory.

And in my opinion, both the free-will theism and the Calvinist explanations are tenable. Though I doubt I would be comfortable doing much of any preaching at the gates of Auschwitz, one could defend both as coherent answers to the problem of evil. As it pertains to the Calvinist explanation, many find great comfort in the belief that the evils they suffer have been inflicted on them by God so they might learn to cling to God in a way they did not and could not before. History is replete with the lives of people who had egregious evils perpetrated against them—rape, maiming, torture, murder—and yet steadfastly believed that it was God who had ultimately done these things to them and that God was still good in doing so.

God Planned My Daughter's Death

"God planned my daughter's death."

This is what Stephen Saint said in his lecture at the 2005 Desiring God National Conference.[24] Years earlier his daughter had died of a massive cerebral hemorrhage that left him emotionally devastated but nevertheless committed to a good God. Saint recounts how his daughter's death enabled him to tap into a passion and love for the lost he could not have otherwise experienced. God planned his daughter's death so that he and many others could better carry out the Great Commission. As Saint poignantly states, "Why is it that we want every chapter to be good when God promises only that in the last chapter he will make all the other chapters make sense, and he doesn't promise we'll see the last chapter here?"[25]

Though much more could be said, this should suffice to show that it is indeed quite possible to reconcile the belief that God ordained the extermination of men, women, and children in the gas chambers of Auschwitz with the belief that God is good, given that God will—in the final chapter—bring about a good so great that all the tears will be wiped away and God will be all in all. Thus, while Auschwitz and evil are a problem, they aren't *the* problem. I could preach Calvinism standing at the gates of Auschwitz.

But could I preach it standing at the gates of hell?

Hell

Few souls are brave enough to let their minds tarry long around the horror of the place we call "hell." For most of Christian history it has been considered a place of eternal torment, a place where teeth incessantly grind in agony, a place where relentless wailing overwhelms the ears, a place where the fire is never quenched and the worm never dies. It's a place where the lines between existence and non-existence blur together as little black holes of self destroy themselves.

Some think it's a place completely absent of the presence of God, while others think it is filled with the searing wrath of God. With varying degrees of success, some have tried to soften this picture of hell. Some affirm annihilationism, the belief that God will simply extinguish the existence of all those in hell.

But no matter how much it is qualified, hell is what it is: a fate so grisly and gruesome that the human mind cannot bear the weight of its terror and nothing else—not rape, not torture, not murder, not infanticide, not Auschwitz—is as much as a blip on the radar compared to it. And as a Calvinist, I found hell left me with a lot of explaining to do.

The Reprobate

The *reprobate*.

This is the technical term used to describe those humans who, according to Calvinism, have been unconditionally predestined to hell. To say it another way, the reprobate are those humans who, before they existed, were chosen by God to spend eternity in hell. And to be clear, the reprobate will spend eternity in hell for sins God ordained they would commit. In summary, then, the reprobate are all those humans who will experience a fate dreadful beyond comprehension (hell) as they are eternally punished by God for sins he ordained they would commit before they existed—*they were created so they could be damned.* If you don't cringe a little, you don't have a pulse.

Some Calvinists find this idea abhorrent and attempt to label it extreme Calvinism, and while I appreciate the sentiment, I don't think it's extreme so much as it is consistent. It is what any Calvinist should believe if she adheres to the notion that God is the all-determining reality (a fundamental tenet of Calvinism). You don't get to have your cake and eat it too. If God is the all-determining reality, then "all" means "all," and those in hell are there because God made certain they would be.[26] I would also note that Calvin, Edwards, and Piper stand by it, insisting that those who shy away from it are wimping out.[27]

This brings us back to preaching Calvinism at the gates of hell.

Tears of the Reprobate

Auschwitz is a problem, but not an unsolvable problem because we can always posit that the suffering God inflicts will be eclipsed by an even greater good for those who trust in him. As John said from Patmos, God will wipe away every tear from their eyes.[28] The end of the story will be so precious that all the hurt will finally make sense. And this is well and good as far as it goes . . .

But how does God wipe away the tears of the reprobate?

What greater good could God bring about for them? How does the final chapter make sense of all the hurt and suffering of the earlier chapters when it ends with a scene of cruelty infinitely beyond anything that has gone before? How are the saints to sing forever of the glory of God while the reprobate whimper and wail because God created them for hell?

As noted earlier, it was not as if this was the first time I had considered the issue of the reprobate. It was a bullet I had long ago bitten: the reprobate are there for the glory of God. But the thing about complex issues is, well, they're complex. They demand continual consideration and reflection: second, third, and fourth looks. And as I began to mull these things over afresh, I didn't like what I saw. I saw someone (me) focusing on the grace shown him to avoid considering the animosity shown others. I saw someone singing the grace of God over the cries of the reprobate. And try as I might, I could no longer muffle their wailing.

When pushed into such a corner in the past, I had leaned on mystery, transcendence, and the Bible, but as I fell back on them, they began unraveling.

The Unraveling of Mystery and Transcendence

Granted, God is above and beyond and need not stringently comply with our moral expectations. Our ideals of love, justice, and goodness do not directly correspond to God's because our ideals are, in a sense, tainted with humanity. That was well and good, but now I was being forced to do some more explaining.

It's fine to say that God's goodness does not *directly* correspond to human notions of goodness,[29] but what exactly could I mean when I said God was good? In what sense was God good if he had done something like creating people so he could damn them? Pardon the pun, but if that is good, what the hell is bad?

And in what sense was God just if he had done something like punishing people eternally for sins he made certain they would commit? How are those in hell merely getting what they deserve when God ordained that they commit their sins? How can humans be held responsible for their sins when God is the ultimate cause of their sins? *Can I come up with a single analogy or illustration that makes the slightest sense of this?*

And how can we say God loves the whole world when he created a good portion of it to go to hell?

It's Like Being Married . . .

I remember sitting in a seminary class listening to a Calvinist pastor take a valiant stab at this last question. Following John Piper, he affirmed that while God loves all people, God doesn't love all people the same.[30] "It's like being married," he said. "I love all women, but I love my wife in a special way that goes far beyond my love for all other women. So it is with God's love for the elect and the reprobate. He loves all people, but he doesn't love all people the same."

I really wanted the analogy to work, but instead of alleviating my anxiety it merely doubled the crushing weight I was feeling. God's love wasn't just different from ours. It wasn't just a "higher" form of love. It wasn't just mysterious and transcendent. *Rather—as far as I could see—it was the exact and utter opposite of our notion of love.* What God called love, we called hate, and there was no way around it. Back to that marriage analogy . . .

It appears to work because when someone tells you he loves his wife in a special way but all women in another way, you (at minimum) assume that his love for all other women includes a genuine desire for their well-being and good. We would expect him to be kind and help them out. And we would certainly expect him to help them avoid some sort of terrible pain and suffering if at all possible. But this is an exceedingly misleading way to speak of God's "love" for the reprobate, for far from helping them avoid terrible pain and suffering, he brings the most terrible pain and suffering upon them (hell).

As such, it would be more truthful to say something along the lines of, "I love my wife by being kind, compassionate, and sacrificial towards her, but I love all other women by doing something far worse than raping, torturing, or murdering them—I ordain their eternal damnation in hell." I suppose I can understand why the pastor did not put it quite like that, but like it or not, this seems to be the strange shape of God's "love" for the reprobate.

The Girl in the Red Coat

In *Schindler's List*, there is a scene involving a little Jewish girl in a red coat. Perched on a hilltop, Oscar Schindler looks down as the Nazis drag Jews out of their homes and murder them. And into this horrific scene walks a little girl.

Your eyes immediately fix upon her because her red coat is the only color in the otherwise black and white scene. With a growing pit in your stomach, you watch as she wanders around—bullets whiz overhead, neighbors are executed inches behind her. We are spared the pain of watching her die on screen, but later on in the movie our eyes fix upon that red coat again as she lies limp atop a pile of dead bodies carried away on a cart. In a movie with so many scenes that stick with you, you just can't forget the girl in the red coat.

My first year in seminary, we had the privilege of talking to a brilliant Calvinist theologian on a conference call. Someone asked him why God causes terrible suffering for people and he responded that he could not really answer that, but believed God would make it up to them in some way. I remember liking the honesty and generosity in his answer, but I couldn't help but ask, "How will God make it up to the reprobate?" He paused for a second, and then replied, "You know, there are certain things that I just don't know but am willing to live with. And that's one of them."

It's an answer similar to the one a good Calvinist friend of mine gives when he is pushed on the reprobate. He believes some people have been elected for damnation, but it's not as if he thinks about them all the time.

Subsequently, he thinks I make too big a deal out of them. Yeah, they're a part of being a Calvinist, but not the only part. Why let them disrupt everything else? Why dwell on them? And to that I can only answer—because you can't forget the little girl in the red coat.

The book of Exodus is kick-started when an oppressed group of slaves cry out in agony, and God hears them. A burning bush, a bunch of plagues, and a parted Red Sea later, and the Israelites stand dancing on the shore because their God is a God who sees oppressive suffering and hears cries of agony—their God is a God who can't forget the little girl in the red coat.

And as Israel's story continues, this fact is borne out again and again and again. God always hears the cry of suffering, and God always sees the oppression of the weak, and God demands that we be a people who do the same.[31] The point here is simple. There is no suffering like that of the damned, no oppression like that of the reprobate, so if you're a Calvinist, you don't have permission to look away. You don't get to treat them like a finer point of eschatology that need not be dwelt on because God teaches us to pay *the most attention* to people like this. If you're going to be a Calvinist, you don't get to forget the reprobate and shame on you if you do.

I fought off my desire to look away and forced myself to hear their cries. I forced myself to remember the little girl in the red coat and reconcile how a good God creates her so he can damn her.

Grasping at Straws

For those who might object that this is going too far, I can only disagree and confess that it seemed Calvinism forced me to call things "good," when they could only be considered the most morally repugnant atrocities imaginable, perpetrated by the Creator himself. Over and over again, I was grasping at straws, offering meaningless analogies as to what I meant when I called God "good" as he did something so (seemingly) reprehensible that my vocabulary strained to describe it.

And that's the thing: there are simply no analogies here, no "well, it's kind of like this," no frame of reference whatsoever. God does things like send the little girl in the red coat to hell forever for sins he predestined her to commit, and yet we're supposed to believe that God is good and even loves her.

Deceive Yourself No Longer

All of this is enough to make many abandon belief in God all together, but that is not an option for many of us. We have seen and experienced too many things to pronounce God dead—his gravity holds us together.

No, rather than disbelieving in God, *the dilemma many face is believing terrible things about God.* In reflecting on the loss of his wife, C. S. Lewis expresses this very sentiment: "Not that I am (I think) in much danger of ceasing to believe in God. The real danger is of coming to believe such dreadful things about Him. The conclusion I dread is not 'So there's no God after all,' but 'So this is what God is really like. Deceive yourself no longer.'"[32]

So this is what God is really like—deceive yourself no longer. For me, this was a fundamental turning point: I could no longer make any sense of the core Christian beliefs in God's love, justice, and goodness. I could no longer deceive myself into thinking I knew what I meant when I said God was good.

I realized the only thing I could say about God was that he did everything for his glory. Seriously—that was it.

God is loving, God is just, God is good—pull back the curtain and all they mean is God does everything for his glory. Or as Professor Quirrell tells Harry Potter, "There is no good and evil, there is only power . . . "[33] God's desire to glorify himself had not only subsumed but consumed all his other desires, so that the only thing I understood about God was that he would glorify himself. Love, justice, and goodness had been warped beyond recognition as they were sucked into the black hole of glory.

Into the Abyss

Did I mention I was still a Calvinist?

Well, I was, and despite the crippling wounds my belief had incurred, I clung to it because—you guessed it—I was convinced the Bible taught it. As John Piper says, "My aim is to let Scripture stand—to let it teach what it will and not to tell it what it cannot say . . . Scripture leads us precisely to this paradoxical position. I am willing to let the paradox stand even if I can't explain it."[34]

And so on the grounds of scripture, I stepped out into the abyss. Who is God? I didn't really know. He glorifies himself—that's all I could say. How did I know? The Bible. But as I stepped into the abyss, the ground crumbled beneath me. Calvinism had pushed God so deep into the void of mystery and transcendence that what happened next was inevitable.

4

God Made Impossible

Across Event Horizon

What would happen if the earth got a little too close to that supermassive black hole at the center of the Milky Way? The technical term for "a little too close" is event horizon: the point of no return. If something reaches event horizon, the next stop is the core of the black hole because at that point its gravity is so strong that escape is impossible. And on that journey to the core, earth would be crushed beyond recognition, a planet filled with unbelievable diversity, crunched together and ripped apart.

At this point in my journey, red flags were waving and my ears threatened to pop from the pressure, but I still let the Bible bring me to the event horizon of Calvinism. And on my descent into the abyss, lines were blurred, diversity flattened, and everything went black.

This is what happens to everything else when everything is about God's glory.

Bible and Belief

God speaks through the Bible. We can go round and round discussing the precise nature of this speaking and whether we should call it infallible or inerrant or something else, but the belief that God is indeed speaking through the Bible is a core Christian distinctive. And yet it is a peculiar irony that belief in the Bible's inspiration and authority has become so ingrained and assumed that many have forgotten that it's just that: a belief. That bears saying again: belief in the inspiration and authority (and whatever other descriptors you feel compelled to tag on) of the Bible is ultimately a belief. And to be more precise, it is the belief that God is truthfully communicating himself and his purposes in the Bible.

Suppose you were asked to prove the inspiration and authority of the Bible—how would you do it? You could point out that archaeological finds corroborate various biblical events, you could highlight the fulfillment of numerous biblical prophecies, you could argue that it makes impeccable sense of the human situation. Or you could go the personal transformation route and speak of how countless multitudes feel they have heard God speak to them through scripture. You could point out that you yourself have experienced the same.

And while these are good reasons to believe in the inspiration and authority of the Bible, every single one of them can be doubted and, more importantly, none of them prove—in any remotely definitive way—either the inspiration or authority of scripture. Sure, some archaeological finds seem to affirm what the Bible says, and some biblical prophecies appear to have been fulfilled, and many people feel God has spoken to them through the Bible.

But none of these things—or anything else that could be mentioned or the cumulative case they could make—could ever give us some sort of objective certainty as to the Bible's inspiration and authority. Think about it: how could you ever be "objectively certain" God speaks through the Bible? What would you even mean? But this is not a knock on the Bible. It's the nature of belief.

Leaping

Somewhere near the heart of belief there is a leap.

For various biblical, rational, and experiential reasons, we are moved towards a given belief. And these reasons can take us a long way and give us great confidence our belief is true, but we can never be absolutely certain of it. No, if you want to truly believe in something—want to act as if it were so, want to incarnate it—then you'll have to jump. It's not a blind leap

(God never asks us to leap blindly), but it is a leap nonetheless. Believing is, after all, risky business.

I have good reasons to believe my wife loves me. She's kind to me, tells me she loves me, respects me, and cooks me the occasional meal. But I cannot be certain she loves me. I cannot "prove" it. Her altruism could simply disguise her nefarious plot to ruin my life. I mean she did say "this" one time, and did "that" the other day. And yet despite the possibility I am wrong, I choose to believe she loves me. I choose to leap and thus to risk being wrong. Of course in a very objective sense, my wife either loves me or she doesn't—it's either true or it isn't. The problem is that as a human being, I am not afforded objective certainty. It belongs to God alone.

It should thus come as no surprise that our belief in the inspiration and authority of the Bible is no exception. Despite the noisy clamoring for the objective certainty of the Bible, such claims—though they could be true—are always beliefs. Call the Bible whatever you want, believe whatever you want about it, but don't fool yourself: you are exercising faith (and lots of it) when you treat the Bible like it's inspired by God. As Lesslie Newbigin says:

> The Bible claims to be a true interpretation of universal history. Since we are not yet at the end of history and since it may yet contain many surprises, we cannot have indubitable certainty. The only possible responses to the claims that the Bible makes are belief or unbelief. There can be no indubitable proofs . . . There is no scientific way of testing the claims and promises that the Bible makes. There is no way of being indubitably certain that this is what history is really about and that this gives us the direction of our lives. It must be, as the church has always said, a matter of divine revelation accepted in faith. [15]

Believing that God speaks truthfully about himself and his purposes in the Bible is, like all belief, a risk. *Belief in the Bible requires belief in a trustworthy God.* And for me, this was *the* problem. Time to connect some dots.

Connecting Dots

What are some things (actions, inclinations) that you would attribute to someone you considered *loving*?

Your list might be pretty long, but I'll bet it comes down to some basic notions about self-sacrifice and genuine concern for the good of others. And at bare minimum, a loving person would not irreparably harm someone he loved, especially when he didn't have to. Furthermore, for a loving person, the issue would never be whether hurting someone else was "fair," but whether it was kind. Can we agree that *from our perspective* (as finite human beings), these things are essential to love?

Now what things you would attribute to someone you considered *just*?

Our lists will vary, but—jumping to the point—your list will likely entail the belief that a just person would not give you a sinful desire, meticulously arrange the circumstances that would lead to you act on that sinful desire, and then stringently punish you for doing that which he had made certain you would do. Right? Especially if the result of all this was not a greater good for you, but just unceasing punishment? Can we agree that from our human perspective, someone who is just doesn't do stuff like that?

Now what are some things you would attribute to someone you considered *good*?

Again, let's jump to the point. You don't think a good person would ever do something like ignore people in terrible suffering when he could easily help them, particularly when he was the ultimate cause of their suffering. Can we agree that *from a human perspective*, someone who is good doesn't do stuff like that?

Million-Dollar Question

Now the million-dollar question.

Can we agree that in light of what God does to the reprobate (creating them in order to damn them), *he does not appear* to have any of these qualities *in any sense analogous* to what we (as human beings) understand them to mean? Can we agree that this act so deeply violates our human understandings of love, justice, and goodness that they *appear* to mean the exact opposite of what we think they mean? Can we agree that God appears to ask us to be more loving, just, and good than he is? If anyone except God did something this brutal and malicious, could you ever bring yourself to call him loving, just, or good? Of course not. And again, we must have the guts to stare this question in the face instead of singing "glory to God" over the cries of the reprobate.

But to be fair, Calvinism has all along been relentless in its affirmation that all this should come as no surprise because God is God and we are humans, so we can't put God in our moral boxes. This is what the Bible teaches, so we have to believe it—but herein lies the rub.

If believing in the inspiration and authority of the Bible requires belief in a trustworthy God who tells the truth about himself, *can Calvinism deliver such a God?* And this is where everything went black.

The Bible Made Impossible

You know what it means to be trustworthy and truthful. It means you can be trusted to tell the truth, especially about yourself. It means the things you say correspond to the way things really are. It means you don't intentionally mislead people. And as I've pointed out, *the Bible is of no use to us unless there is a trustworthy, truthful God speaking in and through it.* And I hope this next question has become so obvious that I need not say it.

If Calvinism is right and we are *so unbelievably wrong* about God's love, justice, and goodness due to our humanity, why would we think we are right about God's integrity and truthfulness in revealing himself in the Bible? In fact, in light of how wrong we (apparently) are about love, justice, and goodness, is it not only possible but probable that we are equally wrong about God's truthfulness and integrity? Why would our ability to understand things like God's integrity and truthfulness be an exception to our otherwise complete rational depravity? Why should they receive a pass? Sure, the Bible says God is truthful and cannot lie, but who are we—as human beings—to assume we know what these things mean? Hasn't it already been proven that we haven't the slightest clue? If we're such imbeciles when it comes to understanding God's morality, and we think lies are bad, then God probably thinks lies are good so he tells us a bunch of lies in the Bible (for his glory of course). As David Baggett and Jerry Walls note:

> If the Bible did indeed teach such a doctrine [unconditional election and reprobation], wouldn't it be more rational to believe that it's not morally reliable? Fundamental to our conviction that scripture is reliable is the trust that God, as perfectly good, would not deceive us. [But] if God is not recognizably good . . . we are not warranted in this trust . . . In the face of this reality, commitment to the truth of biblical revelation gives us powerful reason to reject Calvinist theology.[36]

In a strange turn of events, my Calvinism had taken back the very Bible it had once given me.[37] The theology that had trumpeted the Bible's inspiration and authority had now discredited both. And I realized that if I were to stay a Calvinist, I would no longer know what to do with my Bible.[38] Because if I were to go on treating it like a truthful, reliable revelation of God, it would only be because I didn't have the spine to live out my convictions with consistency.

John Wesley once famously stated that the Bible could not teach the Calvinist doctrine of predestination. According to Wesley, "Whatever . . . Scripture proves, it can never prove this."[39] Previously, I had taken this statement as yet another example of free-will theism's latent humanism and refusal to let the Bible speak for itself. But now I perceived the deeper meaning in Wesley's words. For Wesley, if the Bible teaches that God unconditionally ordains people for eternal damnation, we lose the Bible because we lose a trustworthy God—the Bible becomes impossible. I didn't know how to disagree.

Fade to Black

Luther's search for a gracious God was an important catalyst in the Protestant Reformation.[40] Ironically, I found that I had followed a similar path and was now left searching for a trustworthy, knowable God. The relentless emphasis on mystery and transcendence had completely untethered God from the realm of "knowability." I could not relate to a God whose white was my black. I could fear him, but I could never *know* him—he had made certain of that.

And this is what happened to me at the core of the black hole of self-glorifying deity: *the lights went out and I was left sitting in the dark in an absurd universe with an enigmatic deity of naked power.* C. S. Lewis again captures the essence of the disorientation necessitated by honest, consistent Calvinism:

> Or could one seriously introduce the idea of a bad God, as it were by the back door, through a sort of extreme Calvinism? You could say we are fallen and depraved. We are so depraved that our ideas of goodness count for nothing; or worse than nothing—the very fact that we think something good is presumptive evidence that it is really bad. Now God has in fact—our worse fears are true—all the characteristics we regard as bad: unreasonableness, vanity, vindictiveness, injustice, cruelty. But all these blacks (as they seem to us) are really whites. It's only our depravity that makes them look black to us.
>
> And so what? This, for all practical (and speculative) purposes, sponges God off the slate. The word *good*, applied to him, becomes meaningless: like abracadabra. We have no motive for obeying him. Not even fear. It is true we have his threats and promises. But why should we believe them? If cruelty is from his point of view "good," telling lies may be "good" too. Even if they are true, what then? If his ideas of good are so very different from ours, what he calls Heaven might well be what we should call Hell, and vice-versa.
>
> Finally, if reality at its root is so meaningless to us—or, putting it the other way round, if we are such total imbeciles—what is the point of trying to think either about God or about anything else? This knot comes undone when you try to pull it tight.[41]

I had pulled the knot tight, and now I was being undone. Because if God could unconditionally predestine people to hell—and I was supposed to call this and the God who did it *good*—then my rational equipment was so broken that God was utterly unknowable, and all talk otherwise was whistling in the dark. I could *think* I knew God, I could *feel* I knew God, but I did not *know* God. God and the Bible were impossible, and I was banished to life in a twisted, incoherent universe. Because when everything is about God's glory, everything else—love, justice, goodness, mercy, wrath, meaning, existence—fades to black.

A Wall in Auschwitz

Inside Auschwitz there is a wall.

It's a wall in a cell where people sat in the dark as they awaited execution. And on that wall there is a crude etching scratched into the rock—a man clinging to the waist of Christ. As the lights dimmed, feeble hands scratched against stone, reaching for their Creator.[42]

While few of us have ever been *there*, we have been there: scratching around in the dark, groping for our Creator. But what happens when the God you're reaching for is the one who turned the lights out? What happens when the whole universe fades to black?

I sat in the abyss for a while—hoping my eyes would adjust—but when they didn't I had a decision to make: stay with Calvinism and make this black hole of enigma and "glory" my home, or begin again the painful process of deconstruction and reconstruction that had inaugurated the entire journey. Of course all of this has been a bit dramatic in the sense that it is a tightly condensed narration of a plodding process. As I said at the outset, there are no silver bullets here. Others have walked similar routes, confronted the same problems, crossed event horizon, and don't think the black hole is really that dark. But for me, the onslaught had been too much. Two simple questions:

Who is God?

How do you know?

I could no longer answer either, and so while I didn't know where I was going, I knew black holes weren't fit for staying. I needed a new home.

5

The Crucified God

Leaving Home

My bags were packed, my Jeep was stuffed with belongings, and as I pulled out of the driveway I sensed it was one of those moments where a seemingly insignificant action was a harbinger of a deeper reality: I was leaving home.

Sometimes leaving home is easy, particularly if home has been a place of abuse or neglect. But oftentimes leaving home is difficult, especially if home has been a good place. Of course that is what home is meant to be: a good place, a place where we are loved and nurtured and reminded of who we are. It takes courage to leave a good home, and this is even more the case when you're not sure where you are going. What if your new home isn't as good as your old one? What if it isn't good at all? What if you never find a new home and are left wandering . . . forever? It's enough to make you forfeit your journey for a quick spin around the block.

And while theology is many things for us, it is first and foremost a home.[43] Theology is where we go to be reminded of who God is, who we are, and what we are supposed to be doing. It's the place to which we return at the end of a long day and find our bearings—where we sift and winnow so as to discern where we were but should not have been and where we should have been but were not. When all is muddled, theology reaches down into the mess and finds the beauty below the surface.

Leaving Calvinism was difficult because it had been a good home. It had taken me in when I desperately needed a rescue. It had taught me to prize God's glory above comfort, scripture above my opinions, and a God-centered approach above a human-centered approach. And predictably, my first few steps out the door were a comical affair of wobbly legs and blinded eyes.

I was young, I was restless, and now I was lost.

Limbo

"I just don't know what you believe, and I don't think you do either. It's like you only know what you don't believe."

Years later the words still sting. There I sat, face to face with the youth pastor who had mentored me, loved me, and introduced me to Calvinism, and the conversation was not a fun one. I spent most of it babbling in semi-coherent spurts of frustration and fear, trying to explain why I could not call Calvinism home anymore. I tried to pick it apart, and he listened patiently, asked a couple of questions, and then offered his diagnosis: I was in limbo. I had taken my home apart and now sat like a vagrant on a cold slab of cement. It certainly didn't feel like much of an improvement.

In a clever critique of much critical biblical scholarship, N. T. Wright tells a parable of a man taking his old car into the shop for a tune up.[44] He comes back and finds the mechanic has completely disassembled the car. Parts are strewn all over the garage, and the mechanic goes on and on about how fun it's been taking it apart and how some parts need to be replaced and some renovated. The owner, however, stares in disbelief and then walks away in sorrow. He doesn't need his car dismantled so he can critique and appraise all the pieces. He needs his car tuned up so he can drive it! Some dismantling may well be required, but all the pieces need to be put back together into something that can be driven. The only thing worse than refusing to deconstruct something that clearly needs some deconstructing is deconstructing something and then never doing the hard work of reconstruction.

¡Viva la Deconstrucción!

With sledgehammer in hand, I observed the rubble around me and realized that while the demolition of my home had been necessary, I still needed a place to live. Those who never attempt to find a new home inevitably end up loitering in the dumpsters of cynicism. Cynics love rummaging through other people's trash and airing their dirty laundry for the world to see. If they can't have a home, no one should! Viva la Deconstrucción!

And so I wandered the back alleys for a while, rummaged through my fair share of dumpsters, and vandalized others' homes in an attempt to get people to join me on the streets. Black holes are bad places to live, but the streets aren't much better, so my faith longed for a home.

In recalling this limbo experience, only one word seems adequate: depression. Parker Palmer calls depression a survival mechanism of the soul.[45] It is the soul digging in its heels and refusing to go any further down an unsustainable path. It is the soul warning you that self-destruction awaits if you don't turn around. And for anyone who has experienced depression in any measure, this has more than a ring of truth to it. By the grace of God, I got the memo and began the process of trading in my sledgehammer for nails. But where to start?

God Looks Like Jesus

When starting something, it's good to begin at the beginning. And so what is the theological beginning for Christian faith? Folks smarter than I have offered extensive answers to this question, but I would suggest that the best answer, while profound, is rather simple: *Jesus is God.*

When Jesus of Nazareth stepped on the scene, God himself had taken on flesh. This is of course the great scandal of Christian faith and the subject of the prologue in the Gospel of John:

> In the beginning was the Word, and the Word was with God and the Word was God . . . And the Word became flesh, and dwelt among us, and we saw his glory, glory as of the only begotten from the Father . . . No one has ever seen God. It is God the only Son, who is close to the Father's heart, who has made him known. (John 1:1, 14, 18, NRSV)

In both implicit and explicit ways, this is the relentless affirmation of scripture. The creator God, the liberating God, the God of Israel and the universe, and the God who will return to judge the living and the dead, is the God revealed in the life, death, and resurrection of Jesus the Messiah. As Paul says, "Jesus is the image of the invisible God" (Col 1:15). As Jesus says, "If you've seen me you've seen God" (John 14:9). It's not negotiable, it's not up for debate, and if you don't like it you have to take your ball and go home. God looks like Jesus. Not some of the time, not part of the time, not most of the time, but God has always, does always, and will always looks just like Jesus because Jesus is God.

Jesus to God

This means Christian theology moves *from Jesus to God*, and not from what you think you know about God to Jesus. You find God on Jesus's terms or you find something that isn't God. As Brennan Manning says, " . . . all our prevailing images and understandings of God must crumble in the earthquake of Jesus's self-disclosure . . . If we do not allow Jesus to change our image of God . . . then we cannot profess him as [Lord]."[46] Everything we think we know about God must submit to that which is revealed in Jesus, and when we fail to let God define himself in Jesus because we think we know better, we commit idolatry.

This then is the beginning of Christian faith and theology: a willingness to let Jesus do his work of deconstruction and reconstruction on our hearts and minds so we can know what it means to call him Messiah and God. All of this to say, it would appear scripture not only suggests but demands that we be ruthlessly Christocentric in our theology.

Too Christocentric?

But can we be too Christocentric? Can we focus on Jesus too much?

This is the question pursued by leading Calvinist theologian Bruce Ware and his answer is, in a word, yes: "There is no question, then, of the centrality, supremacy, and finality of the revelation of Jesus Christ. But on the other hand, Jesus Christ should not be viewed as the *exclusive* revelation of who God is."[47]

Ware's point is that Jesus is not the only place God reveals himself. In particular, Ware wants to preserve the witness of the Hebrew scriptures as a place where God is revealed and a place for us to continually revisit if we are to understand what Jesus is showing and telling us. He uses Hebrews 1:1–2 as an example, wherein the writer asserts the supremacy of God's revelation in Jesus but also acknowledges "the rich history or revelation already given when Jesus comes."[48] And his point is well taken.

Theology that locates revelation exclusively in Jesus and implicitly throws away the Old Testament is not only irresponsible but hopelessly thin and in the end fails to take seriously the Jesus it supposedly venerates, because the Jesus of scripture certainly treated the Hebrew scriptures as revelatory. Jesus never taught he was the exclusive revelation of God. But interestingly enough, the crux of the issue comes to a head where Ware's citation of Hebrews 1 drops off.

Hebrews 1:3

Hebrews 1:3, though often overlooked, is one of the most stunning statements in the biblical canon: "And He (Jesus) is the radiance of God's glory and the exact representation of his nature . . . "

The impenetrable mystery of the divine glory blazes like a billion burning stars in the face of Jesus of Nazareth: "We see the glory of God in Jesus, and we see it as it really is."[49] And even more importantly, Jesus is the exact representation of God's nature. Or in the Greek, Jesus is the *character* (exact imprint) of God's *hypstaseos* (being/nature/essence).

This is a loaded phrase, dripping with both moral and ontological implications, with perhaps its most important being the simplest: *the character of Jesus is the character of God.* God would *never* do something Jesus would find morally reprehensible, so if you can't find it in Jesus, then you really ought to think twice before you claim you've found it in God. While it is true that Jesus is not the exclusive revelation of God, it is also true that *Jesus is the exhaustive revelation of God's character, God's heart.*

The Hidden God

One of the least known features of Martin Luther's theology was his doctrine of the *Deus absconditus*, or the hidden God.[50] Going far beyond the obvious truism that not everything about God is comprehensible for humans, Luther believed that standing behind the God revealed in Jesus Christ is a hidden God we know nothing of. In summarizing Luther's doctrine of the hidden God, B. A. Gerrish says, "The image of God does not, after all, *fully* coincide with the picture of Jesus."[51]

Of course from here it's a mere hop, skip, and jump to the doctrine of double predestination, in which the God revealed in Jesus appears to want the whole world to be saved, while the hidden God ordains that many will perish. Although few are as honest as Luther, consistent Calvinism seems to force you into believing in a hidden God.[52]

And while the doctrine of the hidden God denies the teachings of Jesus and Paul mentioned above, one can appreciate the impetus that fueled Luther's thought. In Luther's mind, most of the theology around him domesticated God by cramming him into airtight logical boxes. Understandably, then, Luther wanted to remove the shackles and give God room to be God, and the *sola scriptura* (scripture alone) principle of the Reformation and subsequent Protestant thought have followed suit. We Protestants (supposedly) refuse to put God in any logical or experiential box for fear it will qualify his absolute freedom and thus belittle his glory. We only put him in the Bible box.

But what if the Bible teaches us that God has indeed put himself in yet another box?

God in the [Jesus] Box

And this is precisely what the Bible teaches us about Jesus. We can't put God in a box, but we do not get to decide whether or not God chooses to put himself in one, and in Jesus this is exactly what God has done.

Jesus is the exact representation of God's nature, and there is no hidden God lurking in Jesus's shadow, and we know this because the Bible tells us so. As Dallas Willard says, "Could the character of God really be that of Jesus? The stunning answer is, 'Yes indeed.'"[53] For me, this was an indisputable starting point and the place where deconstruction clocked out and reconstruction clocked in.

So what about Jesus and Calvinism?

Jesus in Black and White

What was Jesus like? What does scripture reveal to us of his character and heart? It must be said at the outset that the question is not as simple as it seems. The so called "quest for the historical Jesus" is an interesting case in point. Biblical scholars pored over the Gospels and often came to wildly different opinions in regards to the identity of the "real" Jesus. Jesus was an egalitarian cynic, Jesus was a Gnostic elitist, Jesus was a good man who liked others and never claimed to be God. Eventually, many were led to the conclusion that searching for the real Jesus was like staring down into a well and mistaking Jesus for your own reflection. When we go to Jesus with an agenda, we tend to find what we're looking for.

On one side, Jesus is often caricatured as a pot-smoking hippie who wouldn't reprimand Hitler for pulling the lever on the gas chamber. As Mark Driscoll notes, many want to "recast Jesus as a limp-wrist hippie in a dress with a lot of product in His hair, who drank decaf and made pithy Zen statements about life while shopping for the perfect pair of shoes."[54] This Jesus could never send anyone to hell because it would violate his fundamental attribute: niceness.

Years earlier, J. B. Phillips made a similar observation in his classic work, *Your God is too Small*, poking fun at meek and mild Jesus:

> Mild! What a word to use for a personality whose challenge and strange attractiveness nineteen centuries have by no means exhausted . . . We hear, or read, of someone who was a "real saint: he never saw any harm in anyone and never spoke a word against anyone all his life." If this really is Christian saintliness then Jesus Christ was no saint.[55]

On the other side, Jesus is often caricatured as a bloodthirsty MMA fighter, doubtlessly engaged in an eternal cage match with the Holy Spirit. After a witty and perceptive assessment of "far left" Jesus, Driscoll continues with his assessment of the "real" Jesus: "In Revelation, Jesus is a pride fighter with a tattoo down His leg, a sword in His hand and the commitment to make someone bleed. That is a guy I can worship. I cannot worship the hippie, diaper, halo Christ because I cannot worship a guy I can beat up."[56]

(Of course the humorous irony here is that Jesus was probably 5'3" and 130 pounds dripping wet—so I'm sure most of us could have beat him up. In fact, he did indeed get beat up pretty badly, and had the audacity to let it be meticulously documented and shared with the whole world. Just see the passion narratives. *So if you cannot worship a guy you can beat up, you can't worship Jesus.*)

Something in between "limp-wrist hippie" Jesus and "Rambo" Jesus must be in order. And so what do we see of Jesus's heart and character when we read the Gospels without an agenda (as best we can), and how should that shape our beliefs for or against Calvinism? The only way to form a good opinion is to read the Gospels.

Gospel Jesus

I've never been able to read the Gospels without cringing a bit. Jesus's words and actions are often a bit prickly. He is terse to his mother, ignores his brothers, won't let prospective disciples bury their dead fathers, tells parables about people being cut to pieces, and makes no bones about the fact that rejecting him will leave you off the guest list at his eschatological block party.[57]

An honest look at the Gospels made it clear to me that Jesus is, well, rough. He has a robust sense of human depravity. He speaks often and clearly about the wrath we are under as a result of it. He lets poor Lazarus spend a couple of days in Sheol for the glory of God. And one day he will come with a sword to judge "the dead, the great and the small."[58] There's no two ways about it, no ifs, ands, or buts: Jesus is rough.

However, the question for Jesus and Calvinism is not "Is Jesus rough?" but "Are the character and teachings of Jesus compatible with the core claims of Calvinism?" Namely, God's creating the reprobate so he could damn them forever. When we look at Jesus, are we attracted to Calvinism or repelled away from it? Or perhaps most to the point, *does the God of Calvinism accurately depict the God revealed in Jesus?*

Twenty-Four

Jesus was somewhere around thirty-three years old when he died. He had a three-year public ministry. John tells us that if one were to write down all the miraculous things Jesus had done, the world itself would not be a big enough library for the resultant collection. And yet with all this material to choose from, all four Gospels unremittingly hone in on one twenty-four hour period as the center and climax of not just the story of Jesus, but the story of Israel, of humanity, and of all creation. It is the twenty-four hours that starts with the kiss of betrayal and ends with the cry of godforsakeness. It is the crucifixion of the Messiah, the Son of God.

And if scripture teaches us to look first and foremost at Jesus in the Gospels, and the Gospels train us to focus in on the crucifixion, it would seem clear that the cross offers us the deepest glimpse into the very heart of God. As Jürgen Moltmann notes, we can see God's hands all over creation, but it is only in the crucifixion that we see God's heart.[59]

This then means that the crucified Jesus is both the *foundation and criticism* of all Christian theology. Christian theology is Christian because it is built up around the crucifixion of God and is continually subjected to merciless interrogation in the shadow of the cross: "For me the crucified Christ became more and more 'the foundation and criticism of Christian theology'. And for me that meant, whatever can stand before the face of the crucified Christ is true Christian theology. What cannot stand there must disappear."[60] Across the theological spectrum, there is remarkable agreement that "the cross is the absolute center of God's revelation to humanity . . . "[61]

And so, *plainly*, does the God on the cross look like the God of Calvinism?

The God on the Cross

Where do you see God as Jesus is being crucified?[62]

Do you see him hovering above the cross, turning away from Jesus, and pouring out wrath? Do you see him in the Roman soldiers crucifying Jesus? Or do you see God precisely in the crucified Jesus, in the God-man nailed to the cross? While it is certainly correct to see God punishing sin as Jesus is being crucified (see Isa 53:10), the Gospels are relentless in their emphasis that we are to see God first and foremost in the Jesus who hangs on the cross. As Moltmann says, "When the crucified Jesus is called the 'image of the invisible God,' the meaning is that *this* is God, and God is like *this* . . . The nucleus of everything that Christian theology says about 'God' is to be found in this Christ event."[63]

That bears saying again—the nucleus of everything that Christian theology says about God is to be found in the crucified Jesus. And in the crucified Jesus, we learn that the God who pours out wrath *is* the God whose hands are nailed to the cross. The God who punishes sin *is* the God who takes the punishment. The God who judges *is* the God who looks upon those crucifying him and says, "Forgive them."[64] I found the crucified God very difficult to square with the God of Calvinism.

Just chew on it a bit. God could have dealt with sin in any way he pleased. God could have done whatever he wanted with us. God could have annihilated us or thrown us into the eternal trash heap. *But God chose the cross.* The Creator dies at the hands of his creation so it (we) doesn't have to get what it deserves. And yet this same crucified God also meticulously planned and carried out the eternal damnation of the creatures he had died for?[65] The God who would stoop so low as to be crucified and buried is the same God doing the eternal crucifying of countless souls for things he made sure they would do? The one who pierces the night air with the cry of godforsakenness on behalf of sinners ordains the godforsakenness of the reprobate?

There had been a time when I stood before the cross stunned by the love, justice, and goodness of God, but towards the end of my journey out of Calvinism, my wonder was replaced with grief. The cross was no longer a place of radiant love and justice, but brutal partiality on the part of the God who supposedly shows no partiality (see Deut 10:17, 2 Chr 19:7, Job 34:19, Acts 10:34, Rom 2:11, Gal 2:6, Eph 6:9).

It was a place where the ultimate absurdity and meaninglessness of the universe came to a head: the God who loves so much so as to suffer crucifixion loves so little so as to glorify himself in the damnation of humans he created to damn. But I was supposed to stand before the cross and worship this ultimately unknowable God of ambiguous morality as if I knew what it meant for him to love me. And if you no longer know how to worship the crucified God, no longer know how to kneel before the cross and say, "Thank you," what do you know?

Divine Schizophrenia

We must further note that the crucified Christ is the same Christ we encounter on every page of the Gospels. What we see at Golgotha is breathtaking and stunning, but for those who have been paying attention, it is not surprising. For from the outset, Jesus has shown himself to be a person who, without exception, enters into the sufferings of others so as to heal and transform them (in Matthew alone see 4:23–24; 8:1–4, 5–13, 14–17, 28–32; 9:1–8, 18–35; 12:9–14, 22–29; 15:21–28, 29–31; 17:14–18; 20:29–34).

Never once do we have any indication that Jesus is the source behind the suffering of others. Rather, Jesus ceaselessly reveals that God is the *healer* of suffering and sickness, not the causer: "Without exception, when Jesus confronted the crippled, deaf, blind, mute, diseased, or demon possessed, he uniformly diagnosed their affliction as something that God did *not* will . . . Jesus consistently revealed God's will for people by *healing them* of their infirmities."[66]

This sets up a rather awkward dilemma in Calvinism wherein God the Father is making people suffer and God the Son (Jesus) is healing people of the suffering the Father is inflicting. How was I supposed to believe God would inflict eternal suffering on people for sins he ordained they commit, when Jesus (the exact representation of God) always healed people of their sufferings? For me this was neither mystery nor paradox, but sheer divine schizophrenia. It opened up a fissure in the very heart of God by splintering the Trinity, setting up Father and Son in opposition to one another—the Father crucifies sinners while the Son is crucified for sinners.

John

But as has been duly noted throughout, there are certainly passages of scripture that can push one towards Calvinism. The most prominent are a few texts from the Gospel of John and of course the infamous Romans 9. John Piper sums up the John passages well:

> We can sum up this great salvation from John's Gospel with the following steps: all that the Father has chosen to be his, he has given to the Son (17:6); and all whom he has given to the Son,

the Son knows (10:14) and calls (10:3); and all whom he calls, know him (10:14) and recognize his voice (10:4–5) and come to him (6:37) and follow him (10:27); and the Son lays down his life for the sheep (10:11,15); and to all for whom he dies he gives eternal life (10:28) and keeps them in the Father's word (17:6), so that none is lost (6:39) or snatched out of his hand (10:28), but is raised up at the last day (6:39) to glorify the Son forever (17:10). This is why the Father has pleasure in election. It is the indestructible foundation for an infallible salvation that redounds in the end to the glory of the Father and the Son.[67]

It's a fair case to be made. But if you're looking for Calvinism in the Gospels, you'll leave parched. You'll hone in on a couple of teachings in John and then project them elsewhere. Again, it's possible—I just don't think it's probable. However, what is probable is that if you go this route, your Bible will become impossible (but we've already been there and done that).

Romans 9

Then of course there is Romans 9, the roaring tiger that devours "free-willers." Cards on the table: do I think Romans 9 teaches Calvinism? No (and we'll get to that in the last chapter). Am I sure about that? No. But here's what I am sure of.

For the first four hundred years of church history, people read Romans 9 and did not think it taught what later came to be called Calvinism. Speaking of Romans 9 and the early Church Fathers, Gerald Bray notes, "Only Augustine, and then only in his later writings, was prepared to accept the full implications of divine predestination."[68] This doesn't mean there is no way Romans 9 teaches Calvinism, but it does mean those closest in chronological proximity to the Apostle Paul did not interpret it in such a way. They all affirmed that election and predestination were based on foreknowledge.[69]

I'm also sure that neither Jesus's teachings nor actions make me feel very comfortable believing in Calvinism. This does not mean there is no way Jesus taught it. But for me, it meant I found it very difficult to believe in something that Jesus did not—in my opinion—clearly teach or live out, and indeed seemed to outright contradict. I felt pretentious staking more on Calvinism than Jesus did.

And as noted earlier, believing in something that is difficult to reconcile with the God revealed in Jesus is not merely logically inconsistent: it's *unbiblical*. Because "Jesus is God" is the most fundamental truth in the Bible, anything I believe that makes Jesus out to not in fact be the exact representation of God's character must be condemned as sub-biblical. It is to presume the revelation of God in Jesus is only half the story, whereas scripture teaches us that Jesus is the whole story. And you can't have it both ways.

You can't have a "crucified-for-sinners God" and a "creates-sinners-in-order-to-crucify-them God." *If you want to be biblical, you can't have a God who is only half like Jesus, because if God is only half like Jesus, he's nothing like Jesus.* So while Romans 9 might be a roaring tiger devouring "free-willers," the crucified Jesus was a mangled lamb that devoured my Calvinism, which brings us to Revelation 5 and a journey to the center of the universe.

Animals, Angels, and a Mangled Lamb

In Revelation 5, John is caught up into a dazzling vision of heaven. There's thunder and lightning and bizarre animals and angels—lots and lots of angels. The hurricane of heaven swirls around John—a barrage of glory and fury, deafening praise and frenetic motion—when suddenly it all ceases. The motion stops, the heavens go silent, and all of creation turns to look because Jesus, the Lion of Judah, the Son of God, the King of the universe is approaching.

And perhaps like little Zaccheus, John climbs on top of a tall angel for a better view, he cranes his neck to see and there—at the throne of heaven, at the center of the universe—is . . . a mangled lamb. The Lion of Judah *is* a mangled lamb. The King of the universe limps to his throne a mangled lamb. Surely there must be some mistake. But as John watches, all of heaven falls down around him, falls down before the mangled lamb, and they begin worshiping him. At the very center of the universe, there is the worship of a mangled lamb.

And it's not a mistake. Twenty-eight times in twenty-two chapters, sword-wielding, conquering, victorious King Jesus is called a lamb (and for those counting, he's called a lion once . . . in the place we're told the

Lion of Judah is actually a slain lamb). And to my Calvinistic chagrin, it was an image I simply could not reconcile.

At the center of the universe, there is not a black hole of deity, endlessly collapsing in on self, but a suffering, crucified, mangled lamb, endlessly giving away self.

Crucifixion Logic

And while a good bit of rational logic brought me here, it was the biblical logic of the crucifixion that brought me to my knees. We can lob verses and logic back and forth until Jesus comes back, but when we gaze at that picture, the real action begins. And as I watched, I realized it was something too big and generous for Calvinism to make sense of. It was the sort of thing that makes you stop arguing because you're too busy worshiping.

I had become a Calvinist because I did not think the Bible left me much of a choice. I began walking away because Calvinism had made both the Bible and God impossible. I took my last steps out the door because I did not think Jesus left me much of a choice, and in the process I had found the foundation for a new home—a home that revolved around the worship of a mangled lamb. Because at the center of the universe, there is and will always be the worship of a mangled lamb.

6

The Glory of God (Is) the Glory of Love

Building a Home

Why do we believe what we believe?

Trying to answer this question is a lot like peeling an onion. We try to cut through all the layers and get to the core, but in the end find there is no fixed core because even at their center, our beliefs have layers. They are a complex interplay of countless factors, of both grabbing on to things that make sense to us and being grabbed by things that would have never made sense had we not been grabbed.

Theology is similar. We make the best possible sense of the possible options. We say *yes* to this and *no* to that. We consult the requisite authorities. We attempt to build a proper theological home for ourselves. And yet forces outside our control are also acting upon us, making sense of us, saying *yes* to us, and building us a theological home of their own. Or so it seems, for when we step back we see that all the disparate pieces and processes have built us a single house.

Such was my experience at least. I had both grabbed and been grabbed by the conviction that the only foundation for theology was the revelation of God in Jesus Christ: "For no man can a lay a foundation other than the one which is laid, which is Jesus Christ" (1 Cor 3:11). Not a theory about the Bible, not a set of presuppositions about how God was supposed to act, but a step of faith wherein I trusted in the revelation of

God in Jesus because the God revealed in Jesus had nudged me to the edge, pushed me over, and caught me. And on this foundation I sought to build a new home.

I visited other places for ideas, even living in them occasionally because my home was not yet fit to be occupied. I gathered materials and thoughts and was gathered by materials and thoughts. I brought my materials and thoughts back home and started hammering away. And in the process the strangest thing would happen. I would spend all day constructing something flimsy, only to wake the next morning and find Someone else had come along and turned it into something both sturdy and beautiful beyond my imagination.

Others have experienced the same. We seek and are sought, we gather and are gathered, we build and are built, and nail by nail a miracle occurs: God helps us raise a new home.

Battle Lines

What is true of history seems to be true of theology: the more things change, the more they stay the same. In every generation there is a (supposedly) mortal battle being waged between liberals and conservatives. The liberals detest the narrow-mindedness of the conservatives, and the conservatives detest the spinelessness of the liberals. Lines are drawn and sides are chosen, and the area in between is no man's land, or better yet, a slippery slope towards the enemy's camp. And of course, both are sure God is on their side.

I am, proudly, a product of the conservative evangelical subculture. And while there have been misdirected detours because of my religious upbringing, I would not have it any other way because through it all I learned a deep sense of reverence for both God and scripture. And it was this reverence that had pushed me into the arms of Calvinism. I realized there was indeed a battle of sorts going on, and at the heart of this battle were two different ways of doing theology.

Do we start from what humans say about God or from what God says about God? Does man get the first word or does God?

If we get the first word, we embark on the hopelessly redundant route of human-centered theology wherein "God" is merely a cipher for our grandest ideals, and a thin, fraudulent notion of love or tolerance is the best we can do for a centerpiece. If God gets the first word, we embark on the unpredictable journey of revelation wherein God is allowed to speak for God's self. And this journey inevitably leads us to the self-glorying, all-determining God of Calvinism. Or does it?

Many who are young and restless end up Reformed because they see no other compelling biblical options—if you say *yes* to glory, sovereignty, and the Bible, you must say *yes* to Calvinism. That's what I thought at least, but now that Calvinism wasn't a viable alternative, where could I turn? Where could I find a faith that was challenging and biblical without making both God and the Bible impossible? Where could I find a theology that made meaningful sense of both glory and love? Where could I find a transcendent, sovereign God who still looked like Jesus, like the God on the cross? And as you might expect, one does not find such a God so much as he finds you.

Barth

Karl Barth is an enigma of sorts. He was a Swiss Reformed theologian who lost his job when he refused to properly swear allegiance to Adolf Hitler, and later sent Hitler a copy of a declaration he had written that vehemently criticized Nazi ideology.[70] His first book, a commentary on Romans, was said to "fall like a bombshell on the playground of the theologians."[71] His magnum opus, *Church Dogmatics*, is one of the largest works of systematic theology ever produced. In April 1962, he appeared on the cover of *Time* magazine, and he is widely recognized as the greatest theologian of the twentieth century. He received a top-notch Protestant liberal education and had a promising future awaiting him in the halls of German Protestant liberalism. But with all this in front of him, he did the strangest thing: he burned the house down.

Liberalism was in the air, subversively infiltrating Christian faith and theology. The Bible was neglected and dismissed as an authority in favor of trending philosophical speculations. Optimism about human progress and goodness was drowning out all talk of depravity. While every generation likes to cry wolf and claim the battle it is fighting is the most important yet, the battle Karl Barth fought has a strong claim to such a title.

After completing his theological education, Barth had imbibed the theology of his teachers and even worked for a leading liberal journal.

But then he went to pastor in the small Swiss town of Safenwil, and as is often the case, his experiences below the ivory tower prompted an audit of his beliefs. His decisive break from Protestant liberalism came when German troops invaded neutral Belgium and the First World War was set in motion. A manifesto was sent around by German intellectuals, supporting this unprovoked act of militancy, and to Barth's horror he found that many of his theological teachers had signed off on it. As Barth says, "I suddenly realized that I could not any longer follow either their ethics and dogmatics or their understanding of the Bible . . ."[72]

He saw the fruit of Protestant liberalism. He saw his old professors supporting the growing German militancy. He saw Jesus disregarded, the cross glossed over, and judgment ignored. He saw the moral impotence of sub-biblical theology. He saw it all and then took a match to it with the simplest and yet most profound of observations: "What does it mean to say that 'God is'? What or who 'is' God? If we want to answer this question legitimately and thoughtfully, we cannot for a moment turn our thoughts anywhere else than to God's act in revelation. We cannot for a moment start from anywhere else than from there."[73]

Over and against liberalism, Barth ferociously affirmed human depravity and the sovereignty of God, insisting that humans cannot come to a true knowledge of God apart from God's revelation to us. It doesn't matter what we think or how we feel—the best of human religious thought unaided by revelation is straw to be burned. What matters is who God reveals himself to be in the act of revelation, and the act of revelation is Jesus Christ. In Jesus, we meet God on his own terms and allow God to speak for God's self. In other words, we meet God in Jesus or we do not meet God at all.

And so what God do we meet in the revelation of Jesus Christ?

He Is the One Who Loves

Previously, I had known that the character of the God revealed in Jesus, the crucified God, did not appear to jibe with the God of Calvinism. What Barth further pointed out was that in the very act of revelation, the act of speaking to humanity and showing himself, God is revealed to be one who freely chooses to share himself with others. God has the right to do with us as he wishes, and God wishes to relate to us. As Barth says:

> God is He who, without having to do so, seeks and creates fel-
> lowship between Himself and us . . . He wills to be ours and He
> wills that we should be His. He wills to belong to us and He wills
> that we should belong to Him. He does not will to be without
> us, and He does not will to be God for Himself nor as God to
> be alone with Himself. He wills as God to be for us and with us
> who are not God.[74]

This is who God is—the One who exists in absolute sufficiency and hap-
piness within himself, and has no need to do anything except be himself
for all eternity. Thus, God does nothing he does not want to do. And yet in
this complete and absolute freedom, God chooses not to exist for himself
alone. God creates and God redeems and God is crucified for creatures
that need not exist. God condescends and forgives and resurrects, and
we find ourselves bowing before an ineffable mystery that we can identify
only because God has given us its name: love.

Self-giving, suffering, crucified love of the Creator poured out on his
creation: "We recognize and appreciate this blessing when we describe
God's being more specifically in the statement that He is the One who
loves."[75]

Love Problems

Western Christianity has a love problem; namely, we have made too little
of love by making too much of it. Love is tolerance, love is inclusion, love
is self-esteem, love is comfort. And in becoming all these things, love has
become nothing: "The term has become debased . . . it has lost its power
of discrimination, having become a cover for all manners of vapid self-
indulgence."[76] For simplicity's sake, let's call this the "soft love" problem: in
becoming everything, love becomes nothing.

During my young, restless, and Reformed years, I thought the rem-
edy to "soft love" was to wholly subordinate the love of God to God's self-
glorification—self-esteem and comfort certainly tend to wilt in the face of
unconditional election. But during my journey out of Calvinism, I came
to believe that while Calvinism did solve the "soft love" problem, it did so
with a painfully ironic consequence.

Whereas "soft love" robs love of meaning by making it everything,
Calvinist love robs love of meaning by making it nothing—or at least

unintelligible. The "love of God" is a hollow phrase, void of meaning and empty on the inside. And while it might be better to let glory co-opt love than tolerance, why settle for either? Why not let love speak for itself, or better yet, why not let God speak for love? Barth agreed and insisted there were five things we needed to know about the love of God.

#1- God (Not I) Defines Love

Did you know that the Book of Acts does not mention love once? Whether you are looking for a noun or a verb, do a word search for "love" and you'll skip straight from John to Romans. Far from being a rhetorical fluke, I think the writer is trying to teach us something: we don't get to define love; God does. And *this* is the first thing we need to know about the love of God. If we want to understand it, then we must go to the place where God defines it: namely, Jesus Christ, crucified. This is the message of 1 John 3:16: "We know love by this, that He laid down His life for us . . . "

It should thus come as no surprise that while Acts does not speak any of love, it is obsessed with telling the story of how a marginal community changed the world through its telling and living the story of a crucified Messiah. Though not in the same doses, this is in some sense true of the whole New Testament witness: *it speaks about crucifixion more than love*. And this is because "What the New Testament means by 'love' is embodied in the cross . . . The content of the word 'love' is given fully and exhaustively in the death of Jesus on the cross; apart from this specific narrative image, the term has no meaning."[77]

We do not get to speak of love abstractly, as some fluffy human ideal of goodwill. We speak of love in the concrete realism of divinity condescending to crucifixion on a wooden stake. We speak of love when we gaze in horror and wonder at the crown of thorns on the brow of the Creator. As Barth says, "Intentionally we have not begun with a definition of love, but with the resolve to let the act of God visible in His revelation speak for itself—God is in His act the One who seeks and creates fellowship with us."[78] This is what we speak of when we speak of the love of God: sovereign, free, self-giving, suffering, crucified love.

#2- God Gives God

Second, in loving us, "God does not give us something, but Himself; and giving us Himself, giving us His only Son, He gives us everything."[79] The greatest thing God can give us is himself. All the things we find so desirable—power, influence, comfort, sex, money—are the unimaginative desires of people who are too easily satisfied. We don't need things. We need God. In loving us, God gives us God.

#3- God's Love Doesn't Take

Third, God does not love us because of something he sees in us, but in spite of what he sees in us. God does not love us because we love him. God loves us because he wants to love us despite the fact that we do not love him. God loves us so that we might come to love him:

> The object of the love of God . . . is another which in itself is not . . . worthy of His pleasure. The love of God always throws a bridge over a crevasse. It is always the light shining out of darkness . . . That He throws a bridge out from Himself to this abandoned one, that He is light in the darkness, is the miracle of the almighty love of God.[80]

This is what we mean when we speak of the unconditional, gracious love of God.

When God looks at us he does not see creatures he should love. He sees creatures that he wants and thus chooses to love despite the fact he should not. And in this, God's love shows itself to be in contradistinction to human love. We love things—God, others, possessions—because of what they can do for us. Moltmann calls this *eros*, a love for the beautiful, and it exposes the bottom-line logic of human love: we love what is beautiful in the hopes it will make us beautiful in return. We love like black holes. We love in order to take.

But this is not the love of God because the love of God does not take—it gives. God does not seek out beautiful objects to love; God makes things beautiful because of his love. After all, the good news of the gospel is not that we are good, but that we are loved:

> But in the cross . . . faith experiences a quite different love of
> God, which loves what is quite different. It loves what is sinful,
> bad, foolish, weak and hateful in order to make it beautiful and
> good and wise and righteous. For sinners are beautiful because
> they are loved; they are not loved because they are beautiful.[81]

#4- God's Love = God's Glory

Fourth, God's love is an end in itself. And here I found a radical departure
from Jonathan Edwards, John Piper, and the self-glorifying black hole of
Neo-Calvinism. Edwards claimed that the ultimate aim of God in creating
the world was the full manifestation of his glory (i.e., his self-glorification).
Love is just a cog in the bigger glory machine.

Not so for Barth: "Certainly in loving us God wills His own glory . . .
But He does not love us because He wills this. He wills it for the sake of
His love. God loves in realizing these purposes. But God loves because He
loves; because this act is His being, His essence and His nature."[82]

God doesn't love us in order to take something from us (glory, worship, praise)—that's what needy, greedy, human love does. *God loves because he loves*—the only love in existence that doesn't need a reason.

And so when God opens his heart to us and we get a glimpse of
what makes it beat (Jesus Christ crucified), we see a desire to love at all
costs, not glorify himself at all costs. That said, it would be a mistake to
think you must choose between God's love and glory because God wills
to glorify himself as the God who, freely and sovereignly, loves at all costs
(see Deut 7:8, Jer 31:3, Isa 63:9, John 3:16, Rom 8:31–39, Titus 2:14, Phil
2:5–11, Rev 5:6–10). As Miroslav Volf says, "We don't have to give up on
the idea that God seeks God's own glory. We just need to say that God's
glory, which is God's very being, *is* God's love . . . In seeking God's own
glory, God merely insists on being toward human beings the God who
gives."[83]

When we speak of the glory of God, we speak of the God who gave
himself to us, to all of us, in Jesus Christ. *Love is not just a cog in the glory
machine*. The glory of God *is* the glory of love.

#5- Necessary and Free

Fifth, God's love is both necessary and completely free. And here all the horizons of the love of God converge. From all eternity God is the being who has existed in perfect, glorious, self-giving love among Father, Son, and Spirit. Before we existed, God loved. From all eternity God has loved because love is who God is. God, infinite and eternal, is the God of love. As such the love of God is necessary in the sense that God has to be himself.

But God's love is completely free in the sense that he is merely being who he is. If God, at his very core, is a person(s) of infinite self-giving love, then even though God cannot be something else (hateful, arbitrary) this is no limitation: "To be moved by oneself in love is to be divinely free."[84] In fact, this is the freedom only God has: "But freedom in its positive and proper qualities means to be grounded in one's own being, to be determined and moved by oneself. This is the freedom of the divine life and love."[85]

Thus, far from limiting God or undermining his glory, God's love is the ultimate expression of his freedom, sovereignty and glory. His transcendence is exhibited supremely in the fact that though God is utterly unconditioned, he reaches outside himself to create and bind himself to others—a transcendence characterized by outwardness and not inwardness.

The gravity of God's glory is rooted in his *giving*, not his taking, and so God's glory shines brightest in his existence as the only non-black hole of self in the universe—the One who in absolute freedom loves absolutely.

Relocating the Mystery

I came to the end of this devastatingly merciful vision of the love of God and realized the mystery of God had not been removed; it had been relocated. No longer was the mystery how a good God, how the God revealed in Jesus, how the crucified God, could create people in order to damn them. The mystery is not in some hidden God lurking behind Jesus, but in Jesus.

The mystery is that *God* is damned in order to save. The mystery is that in his absolute freedom, God puts on flesh, goes up on the cross and down into the grave. The mystery is that the heart of God is filled with an infinite supply of the self-giving, redemptive, reconciling energy we call love. The mystery of God is that he loves us—all of us.

> "God is" means "God loves" . . . All our further insights about who and what God is must revolve round this mystery—the mystery of his loving . . . The consideration of the mystery of His freedom cannot lead us in any other direction. It cannot lead us to another god who is not the One who loves . . . Everything will depend on our not losing the basic definition we have now found, that God is the One who loves.[86]

"God is" means God—in absolute, sovereign freedom—loves. This is compelling. This is glorious. This is biblical. This is the God revealed in Jesus: a completely free, sovereign, and transcendent God who chooses to give himself away in love on a cross. What in the world would move God to do such a thing? He tells us to call it love. It's the real mystery.

Jesus Love Me, This I Know

Having let God speak for himself, I had found—or been found by—an infinitely glorious God, but it was not the God of Calvinism. It was the sovereign, self-giving, suffering, crucified God of Jesus Christ. It was the God who does not need us but does not want to be without us—not because we deserve it, but because it's just who he is. And for me, this was a glory far beyond that of the self-glorifying God of Calvinism.

And this brings us back to Karl Barth. Towards the end of his life, he made his one and only trip to America, lecturing at Princeton Theological Seminary and the University of Chicago. Legend has it that at some point Barth was asked to summarize the meaning of the millions of words he had written. He thought for a moment and then said:

"Jesus loves me, this I know, for the Bible tells me so."

7

Free Will, Kenosis, and a Peculiar Kind of Sovereignty

Free Will

Perhaps you have noticed that up until now I haven't said a thing about free will.[87] And that is because it has both nothing and everything to do with why I left my Calvinist home and went searching for a new one.

As alluded to in the first paragraph of the first chapter, belief in free will is no foundation on which to build a theological home, *though this is the unfortunate mistake of many.* For starters, you can never be sure that you actually have free will because there is no way to know if you could choose to do other than what you actually chose. In other words, while we experience ourselves as having free will, we can never be sure if we really do. But more importantly, to begin with free will is to do theology from the bottom up. It is to begin with what you supposedly know about humans and work to what must then be true of God. As Bruce Ware says:

> When the starting place for understanding the God-world rela-
> tionship is the uncontested reality of libertarian free will, then
> God must be understood in a matter that "fits" our freedom . . .
> We begin with what we know to be true about human beings.
> We know that we are free . . . Therefore, all else that we say about
> God and any other theological subject must be understood in a

manner that accords with, and does not contradict, libertarian freedom.[88]

And on this point, Ware, a Calvinist, and any thoughtful free-will theist would agree. Theology cannot start from human reason or experience, and if it does we will find that we have merely created God in our own image. This is the house Barth burned down.

So when it comes to free will, the question is not "Do you think you have free will?" but "What does God say about free will?"

Chicken or the Egg?

Looking for free will in the Bible is like looking for gravity: it's assumed everywhere and holds everything together, so you probably won't notice it until it's missing and you float away.

This is why it's usually easier to rattle off multiple verses that seem to contradict free will than it is to name a single verse that affirms it. We think of God hardening Pharaoh's heart because the passage sticks out—it cuts against the grain of the rest of the biblical narrative. We don't think of the sixty-three times Jesus tells people to do or not do something during his Sermon on the Mount, seemingly assuming they had the ability to do or not do what he said, because it flows seamlessly with the pattern of the biblical narrative.[89] But to be fair, there are many verses on both sides, so the issue usually comes down to the familiar dilemma regarding priority of order.

Which came first, the chicken or the egg? Are we to read the free-will texts in light of the determinism texts and thus assume that all the evidences of free will in scripture are a charade? Or are we to read the determinism texts in light of the free-will texts and thus assume that all the apparent negations of free will are rare and unique exceptions to the normal way God does things?

In other words, does free will or determinism serve as the backdrop of the biblical narrative? In pursuing such a question, we would do well to start where the story starts.

In the Beginning

Barasit.

It's the first word in the Bible and, fittingly, means "in the begin-ning."[90] And that's what Genesis is about: beginnings and origins. A long story, full of twists and turns, tears and triumphs, will come after it. But like most good stories, it doesn't make any sense if you don't know how it begins. And so it begins.

The curtain is drawn on a scene of God sitting quietly in the dark. He steps out onto space and then it happens. The creative spark that will soon spin out a universe is ignited in the divine heart and creation is set in motion: "Then God said, 'Let there be light', and there was light" (Gen 1:3). And then there are heavens and earth and seas, sun and moon and stars, birds and fish and trees—day one, day two, day three, day four, day five—and it is all good. God rules in complete sovereignty over an idyllic world, and this makes what happens next all the more puzzling.

A new character is introduced, and the nature of his existence is rather bizarre. God reaches down, grabs a handful of dust, breathes into it, and human life begins. And this is what humans are: walking piles of dust animated by the breath of God. So now there is God and humans, and the stage is set for the circuitous epic that follows, but not until we learn the terms of the divine/human relationship. In creating humans, just what has God done?

Imago Dei

Genesis 1:26–28 reads:

> Then God said, "Let Us make man in Our image, according to Our likeness; and let them rule over the fish of the sea and over the birds of the sky and over the cattle and over all the earth, and over every creeping thing that creeps on the earth." God created man in His own image, in the image of God He created him; male and female He created them. God blessed them; and God said to them, "Be fruitful and multiply, and fill the earth, and subdue it; and rule over the fish of the sea and over the birds of the sky and over every living thing that moves on the earth."

One of the deepest of biblical truths is that of the imago Dei: humans have been created in the image of God. But what does this mean? Opinions vary and some are better than others, but if we want to think biblically about the imago Dei, then we must think in the terms and images Genesis 1:26–28 provides: our ruling over God's creation as God's creatures.

In the ancient Near East, it was commonly believed that a king was an image or representative of his god(s), ruling on their behalf. The gods would grant the king power and authority to rule. As Walter Brueggemann says, "It is now generally agreed that the image of God reflected in human personality is after the manner of a king who establishes statues of himself to assert his sovereign rule where the king himself cannot be present."[91]

But unlike their ancient Near Eastern neighbors, the Hebrews believed that not only the king but all humanity had been created in God's image.[92] All humanity had been entrusted with the task of ruling God's creation as God himself would rule it. The implication is plain: within certain limitations, *God empowers us to rule as he rules and this is what it means to have been created in his image.* The image we bear is that of a power-sharing God, and the first words ever spoken about humanity are a divine invitation to share in his power, authority, and rule.

To say this all another way, God creates the world as his kingdom. But in a strange turn of events, God creates humans and carves them out their own little provinces in the midst of his kingdom, entrusting them with a tiny sliver of reality. As Psalm 115:16 says, "The heavens are the heavens of the Lord, but the earth he has given to the sons of men." God is still sovereign—for all creation is his kingdom—but he grants a limited amount of freedom and control to others. So in the very act of creating humans and not something else—more fish or birds—God chooses to share some of his power and sovereignty: "The initiative has been solely God's, but once the invitation has been issued, God establishes a power-sharing relationship with humans."[93] It is a revolutionary idea.

Far from being another power-grabbing, insecure, anxiety-ridden god of the ancient Near Eastern pantheons, *the Creator God is so secure and free that he has the power to give power away.* He is not anxious about his rule or insecure about his sovereignty. He does not grab or hoard—he gives. And the story continues.

Trees

There are lots of trees in the Garden of Eden, but two are singled out: the tree of life and tree of the knowledge of good and evil.[94] Adam is told he can eat from every single tree . . . except the tree of the knowledge of good and evil.[95] And in one of humanity's timeless tales, Adam does just that, sending creation spiraling out of control, in the wake of which we are often left asking why. Why did Adam eat from the one tree he was told to stay away from? And yet there is an even deeper why question: why does God even put that tree in the garden? Why give us the opportunity to smear his good creation? Why not make a safer garden? This brings us back to the divine invitation that welcomed humanity into the world.

You can almost picture it. The tree of life and the tree of the knowledge of good and evil stand side by side. Adam exists by the generosity and graciousness of God and while his existence has an astounding range of freedom, it also has limits. Adam has the freedom to eat from the tree of the knowledge of good and evil, but if he does so he will die. So as Adam stands before these two trees, he stands before the crux of the divine/human relationship. He is free to live within or outside of God's will, but if he chooses to live outside it, he will undo his own existence.

For while he has a range of independence, his existence is still completely dependent upon his Creator. It is a relationship of *independent dependence*. As Nahum Sarna says, "The human race is not inherently sovereign, but enjoys its dominion solely by the grace of God."[96] Human freedom is intended to be exercised in a relationship of complete dependence upon the graciousness of God, and when we opt out of grace we opt in to death. And this reminds us of yet another tree.

God hangs on a tree. Thousands of years have passed since Adam's decision to have existence on his own terms, and all subsequent humanity has followed suit. The tree of life is gone. We have turned in on ourselves and we will not choose God (total depravity). But instead of giving up on the design implemented in Eden, instead of leaving us to our depravity, God does the unthinkable: he offers another tree, a tree that will both forgive us our sins and heal us of our sinfulness, if we will surrender ourselves to the grace of God.

Jesus hangs on the cross saying, "Father, forgive them; for they do not know what they are doing" (Luke 23:34). Years later the apostle Paul will look at the cross and say, "Therefore, we are ambassadors for Christ, as though God were making an appeal through us; we beg you on behalf of Christ, be reconciled to God" (2 Cor 5:20). The Creator hanging on a tree, begging us to be reconciled him, re-issuing the divine invitation to exercise our independence in complete submission to our utter dependence upon him. And this reminds us of yet another tree.

The story has come to an end. All the wayward, rebellious kingdoms of the world have been confronted and crushed by the kingdom of God.[97] Those who have refused to cede their kingdoms to the crucified God now receive the death and judgment looming since Genesis 3. But those who have surrendered their rule and embraced their dependence now receive their promise. Tears are wiped away, death is put to death, and the kingdom of God is all in all.[98] And in the middle of this resurrection kingdom, there is a tree:

> Then he showed me a river of the water of life, clear as crystal, coming from the throne of God and of the Lamb . . . On either side of the river was the tree of life, bearing twelve kinds of fruit, yielding its fruit every month; and the leaves of the tree were for the healing of the nations. There will no longer be any curse; and the throne of God and of the Lamb will be in it, and His bond-servants will serve Him . . . And there will no longer be any night; and they will not have need of the light of a lamp nor the light of the sun, because the Lord God will illumine them; and they will reign forever and ever. (Rev 22:1–5)

The story ends with God's people reigning in joyful submission forever and ever and ever. Those who have accepted the divine invitation to be truly human, to be redeemed and to freely submit to their Creator, now eat from the tree of life. And it is all of grace—a gift of the God who, in absolute freedom, chooses to love absolutely.

Biblical Free Will

When we step back from all this, we see that from beginning to end and everywhere in between, the Bible is the story of a graciously peculiar God who, fittingly, exercises a peculiar kind of sovereignty over his creation: "the divine sovereignty in creation is understood, not in terms of absolute divine control, but as a sovereignty that gives power over to the created for the sake of a relationship of integrity."[99]

Although God has every right to issue only commands, he often issues invitations. God is always sovereign, but that means he—and not we—gets to decide what shape that sovereignty takes. And apparently, God's sovereignty makes room for human freedom so that God and humans can have a personal, and not merely causal, relationship. If God had wanted it otherwise, one suspects he would have just rested on the sixth day instead of the seventh. But this is the paradox of love. As N. T. Wright says:

> God's creative love, precisely by being love, creates . . . space for there to be things that are genuinely other than God . . . This is part of the paradox of love, in which love freely given creates a context for love to be freely returned, and so on in a cycle where complete freedom and complete union do not cancel each other out but rather celebrate each other . . . [100]

And it is only once we have anchored ourselves in scripture that we can speak meaningfully and biblically of free will. Far from being an invention of human logic and deduction, free will grounds and permeates the biblical narrative.

Begin at the Beginning

But as noted earlier, there are certainly other ways to read the biblical story. You could argue that God actually pre-determined the events in Eden and that God never surrenders any of his control over creation. As Bruce Ware says:

> The sole criterion for understanding the nature of divine sovereignty is simply this: whatever God tells us in Scripture about his lordship and sovereign rulership over the universe is what we should believe . . . From the beginning of the Bible to the end (quite literally), readers are constantly encouraged, in account after account, to think of God as in control of what takes place in the world.[101]

But this is a reading that, in my opinion, fails to do precisely what Ware claims it does: begin at the beginning. It is a reading that begins in Romans

9 or Ephesians 1, and proceeds to read the rest of the biblical narrative from a beginning that is not the beginning God gives us. For example, after making his claim that the Calvinist definition of sovereignty is taught from the beginning of the Bible, Ware begins with an exposition of . . . Ephesians 1:11.[102] I think we can agree this is not the beginning. I did and still do find a Calvinist reading of scripture that denies genuine free will possible, but I no longer find it the best reading of the Bible.[103]

The Shape of Sovereignty

At this point many of our notions of sovereignty have been inverted and twisted out of joint, and Piper puts his finger on our discomfort: "Non-omnipotent omnipotence is a self-contradiction."[104] In other words, "God cannot use his sovereignty to make himself unsovereign."[105] The idea is that God cannot help but be in complete control, cannot check his power, and "God is sovereign" means "God is in complete control."

But to state the obvious, "God is sovereign" does not have to mean, "God is in complete control," from either a biblical (as we have seen) or logical perspective. Rather what Piper—and many others—does is smuggle his definition of sovereignty into the word *sovereignty*. For Piper, sovereignty is the absolute use of absolute power and absolute control at absolutely all times. And according to such a definition he's right, but this definition is neither biblically nor logically necessitated. And of course far more importantly, it seems somewhat incongruous with the biblical definition of sovereignty. As Greg Boyd states:

> Why should we assume that God desires to do everything he has the raw power to do? . . . Scripture makes it evident that though God *could* control us, he desires to empower us to be self-determining, morally responsible agents. "Whatever the Lord pleases he does," *including* creating free agents.[106]

Or to put it another way, who says God can't be sovereign over his sovereignty? Not God.

As such, to claim that God voluntarily and temporarily limits his sovereignty to allow for free moral agents is not to disfigure God's sovereignty in a humanistic attempt to make it more palatable. Rather, it is to let God's sovereignty speak for itself as opposed to us telling it what it has to mean. And when sovereignty speaks for itself, it is clear that its shape is kenotic.

Kenosis

I'm not sure anything tells us more about who God is than the great Christological hymn of Philippians 2:

> Have this attitude in yourselves which was also in Christ Jesus, who, although He existed in the form of God, did not regard equality with God a thing to be grasped, but emptied Himself, taking the form of a bond-servant, and being made in the likeness of men . . . He humbled Himself by becoming obedient to the point of death, even death on a cross.[107]

God the Son, creator and sustainer of the cosmos, empties himself. The Greek word is *ekenosen,* and it carries with it the notion of a giving away, a voluntary laying down of something that is rightfully yours. Jesus, though fully God and thus possessing all the rights and privileges of the Creator, chooses to give these things away. We call this kenosis. According to Paul, as Todd Still writes:

> Jesus did not view his divine status as something to be protected or preserved. In contradistinction to self-consumed rulers and despots, he did not regard his lofty state as a perch from which to look down upon others as he "ruled the roost" and did whatever he will-nilly well pleased . . . Far from tenaciously grasping or indiscriminately exercising his divine privileges and prerogatives, Jesus divested himself of his divine position, prestige, and perks.[108]

Among the many truths we can glean from the Incarnation is the truth that God most certainly can and does check his sovereignty for the sake of his creation. And even more so, the truth of the great kenotic hymn is that Jesus does not cease to be like God in this act of voluntary self-limitation. *Rather, it is in this act of voluntary, gracious self-giving and self-limitation that Jesus most reveals what God is like,* for this is what God has been doing from the beginning. The God who limits his sovereignty by creating humans in his image is the God who limits his sovereignty as he lies in the manger. The God who shares his sovereignty by placing the tree of the knowledge of good and evil in Eden is the God who shares his sovereignty as he hangs on the tree at Golgotha.

To be clear, God can be as in control as he wants to be, and scripture certainly leads us to believe that *God can and often does intervene decisively*, even manipulating circumstances to bring about his will. But God has willed that he will not necessarily always get his way.[109] God has willed that there be other wills that matter. From creation to cross to new creation, God limits himself, not because he has to but because he wants to. And apparently, God wants to love and be loved more than he wants to be in complete control: "Omnipotence can indeed be longed for and worshipped by helpless men, but omnipotence is never loved; it is only feared. What sort of being, then, would be a God who was only 'almighty'? He would be . . . a being who is loved by no one."[110] Roger Olson sums up God's self-limiting sovereignty well:

> Doesn't this limit God's power and sovereignty? No, because God remains omnipotent; he *could* control everything and everyone if he chose to. For the sake of having real, personal creatures who can freely choose to love him or not, God limits his control. Still, God is sovereign in the sense that nothing at all can ever happen that God does not allow. Nothing falls totally outside of God's supervening oversight and governance.[111]

Resistance Is Futile

When faced with this peculiar sovereignty of our God, we have a couple of options. We can resist it. We can say it is audacious to think God would give over so much control to humans. We can say it is beneath God to limit himself and that those who believe such belittle God's glory. We can insist God is a black hole. And while I understand such sentiments and have shared them myself, I only know one way to respond: take it up with God. Because apparently, God doesn't think it is beneath him to share his sovereignty. Apparently, God's glory does not necessitate his hoarding of all the power in the universe.

And here we find a bit of an irony. As a Calvinist, I labeled free-will theism humanistic. I thought the God of free-will theism was merely a projection of human ideals and concepts, and this is often the case. However, the same accusation can be made of Calvinism.

A ruler who absolutely, unequivocally exerts the full measure of his control at all times, leaving no room for dissension or contrary wills? That's not the most divine thing I've ever heard—sounds like little black holes of self projecting a supermassive black hole of Self into the heavens.

I say that tongue in cheek, merely highlighting the fact that Calvinist sovereignty is neither more "glorious" than self-limiting, kenotic sovereignty nor immune to accusations of projection. The fact is, we all do a little projecting. One hopes God will forgive us. And that brings us to the second way we can respond to the peculiar sovereignty of God.

Strange Enough to Be True

C. S Lewis once said that Christianity's peculiarity aided in his conversion. Its stories and beliefs were so odd, they struck him as something humans wouldn't have made up. They struck him as something just strange enough to be true.[112]

I feel the same about God's self-giving sovereignty—we could not have guessed it, would not have made it up, and that's good. It means it's strange enough to be true. It sounds like something *God* would do. It sounds like a chance to surrender to the ways of a God who, thankfully, is not like us.

8

Monsters in the Basement

Monsters in the Basement

A rugged pilgrimage had come to an end. Belief that had flickered now shone bright. Faith that had been dormant sprouted anew. A lost soul had again been found. The process of deconstruction and reconstruction had caused doubt and despair, but it had also given me a new place to lay my head. I was tired and I was weary but I knew I was home. It was a home founded on the glory of a crucified God of self-giving love, and around that center had sprung up walls of grace, free will, kenosis, and a peculiar sort of sovereignty. And in my opinion, it was quite a home.

But no home is perfect. There are always hidden cracks, a leaky faucet, a squeaky board. Sometimes there are strange noises coming from the basement. As such, finding a home is not a matter of discovering the perfect home so much as it is finding a place you love and then learning to live with its frustrations. It should then come as no surprise that once the novelty of my new place wore off, I began to notice some cracks and some leaks. I even began to hear some noises in the basement.

And so what does one do with the cracks, the leaks, and the noises? How do we handle the potential monsters down in our basement? Do we cover them up and try to convince ourselves and others they aren't really there? Such is the usual course of action. But such a course does not serve the truth, for the truth is never afraid of honesty. The truth isn't worried about winning an argument or creating a massive following. The truth just wants to come out into the light.

And so that's what I, to the best of my ability, did. I went down to the basement, rounded up all the monsters, and then dragged them out into the light and learned to live with them.

Parking Can Be a Nightmare

My trip down to the basement of free-will theism was set in motion my last year of college. A representative from a nearby seminary had come on a recruiting visit, and so he did what representatives on recruiting visits do: he told us how perfect his school was. It had top-notch academics, top-notch spiritual formation, top-notch campus life, and the professors and students were often seen skipping through the hall together. You know the drill. You get an embarrassingly positive sales pitch in which every strength is highlighted and no weakness is acknowledged. The side effects are always in fine print. And while such a tactic might be persuasive, it doesn't exactly help you make a good decision.

So I raised my hand and asked him, "What is the worst thing about your seminary?" You could tell it was one of those questions he was not prepared for. He wanted to avoid saying anything negative about the school, but realizing he had no elegant outs, he reluctantly said, "Well I've never been asked that question before, so I guess if I had to say something . . . parking can be a nightmare." Very helpful.

This maddening situation of semi-transparency is the unfortunate reality of most theological sales pitches. Theological realtors are often more concerned with selling you a home just like theirs than they are helping you find the right place for you. But talk is cheap and while complaining feels good, it usually doesn't accomplish much, so those of us who want more theological honesty must lead the way by openly acknowledging the holes, gaps, and monsters in our theological constructs.

We have to let others see the mysteries we are learning to live with.

Two Kinds of Free Will

Both Calvinism and free-will theism affirm free will and yet define it completely differently.

Calvinist free will is called compatibilism, and it means that you are free so long as you are doing what you want. As long as you are acting on your strongest inclination, you are free, regardless of whether or not you could do otherwise. Hence in Calvinism, God can unilaterally determine your inclinations so that you must do what he ordains for you to do, and yet you still "freely" do it. So if God determines that you will want to reject Jesus, you are still freely rejecting him—even though God determined it and you could not have done otherwise—because you were doing what you wanted. This is how Calvinists typically explain the fall: God foreordained Adam and Eve's sin, but they still sinned freely because they were doing what they wanted.

Confused? If so you're in good company because confusion is what happens when you use a term so counter-intuitively.

Free-will theism's understanding of free will is called libertarian freedom and it means the power of contrary choice. You are free if you have the ability to choose between two or more things. This doesn't mean your freedom is absolute, for our choices are always far more conditioned than we could ever imagine. But it does mean that in order for us to have genuine free will, we must be able to act on various inclinations and not just our strongest.

Mexico or Sweden

And while compatibilism (Calvinist "free will") is troublesome for a number of reasons already mentioned (the existence of sin, evil, and hell), it must also be admitted that the greatest mystery of free-will theism is the mystery of libertarian free will. Indeed many philosophers find the very idea of libertarian free will incoherent.

Consider this: you want to go on vacation and have narrowed your choices down to Mexico and Sweden, and after much deliberation you decide on Mexico. Now according to libertarian free will, the exact same set of circumstances and deliberations (same desires, same inclinations, same beliefs, etc.) that led you to choose Mexico could have also led you to choose Sweden. This seems rather odd. If nothing were changed, where would this decision to choose Sweden come from? Did it bubble up magically from thin air? Did it materialize in your pre-frontal cortex? How can you make any sort of sense of this "free" impulse?

This accusation is fair enough, but any thoughtful Christian will realize that if God's creation of the world was an act of grace, then God must have had the ability not to create the world. And if this is true, then at minimum, God must have libertarian freedom. And if God has libertarian freedom, then even though we cannot fully (or remotely) explain it, the fact that God has it means it is not an incoherent or absurd idea.

Sin

Now lest we think this is just a game of sophomore philosophy, here is where the rubber begins to meet the road. Where did the first sinful impulse come from?

Although consistent Calvinists believe that God ordained the fall, they hesitate to say that God put the first sinful impulse in Adam. But if it didn't come from God, where else could it have come from? Critiques of Calvinism accuse it of inconsistency here. It has already affirmed that God is the all-determining reality and ordained the fall, and yet it won't just bite the bullet and admit that God ordained the first sinful impulse in Adam. What do Calvinists have to say for themselves? They appeal to mystery: "We don't know where the first sinful impulse came from." But it sure doesn't sound like they don't know where it came from so much as they don't want to say where it came from. Or better yet, it sounds like they willfully suspend the logic of their theology at this point.

But now we must ask the same question of free-will theism: where did the first sinful impulse come from? God creates a sinless world and then creates sinless humans. How does a sinless human in a sinless world choose to sin? Where does the impulse come from? Appealing to Satan doesn't really help because then we just have to ask the same question of Satan: where does his first evil impulse come from? Indeed in the end the best thing we can say is, "It's a mystery." We don't believe God ordained it, we do believe Adam is responsible for it, but we can't explain how a sinless creature chooses to sin.

Salvation

But now let's move from talking about sin to talking about salvation. According to free-will theism, why do some people accept Christ while others reject him? It's certainly not because those who accept Christ are—in some moral sense—"better" than those who reject him, for we are all totally depraved apart from the grace of God. So what then? What have we free-will theists to say for ourselves? It's a mystery. As Jerry Walls notes:

> Notice that both Calvinist and free will theologians ultimately arrive at a point where further explanations are impossible. Both reach the limit of finally inexplicable choice. The free will theologian cannot fully explain why some choose Christ while others do not. The Calvinist cannot tell us why or on what basis God chooses some for salvation and passes others by.[113]

Free-will theism must learn to live with the inexplicable choice of salvation. We cannot explain why some surrender to the grace of God and others don't.

But if you're like me, while these mysteries of free will, the first sin, and salvation are certainly puzzling, they don't bother me too much. In fact, they seem rather appropriate. They seem to be biblical mysteries that don't make the Bible or God impossible and I am willing to live with those. But let's press the mystery of salvation a bit further because a good number of Calvinists think free-will theism's understanding of salvation inevitably leads to the unforgiveable sin: stealing God's glory.

Boasting in Heaven

So a Calvinist and a free-will theist stand before the pearly gates and Saint Peter asks them, "Who gets the glory for your salvation?" The Calvinist quickly responds, "God gets all the glory because my salvation is all his doing. Per Ephesians 1, he elected me before the foundation of the world, justified me on the cross, and ordained that I would believe in and accept Jesus." Satisfied, Saint Peter then turns to the free-will theist, who says, "Well, God gets 99 percent of the glory because he did all the heavy lifting, but then I chose to believe and accept Jesus so I'll just take 1 percent." Saint Peter gasps in horror, raps the free-will theist over the head with his golden scepter, and says this is just another example of how free-will theism steals God's glory. It creates people who would boast in heaven.

This is the typical charge leveled against synergism, which is the technical term for the libertarian understanding of salvation in which there is divine/human cooperation in salvation—God, in grace, does everything but humans have to cooperate by accepting this grace. According to people like James Montgomery Boice, free-will theists cannot give God glory: "They want to glorify God. Indeed, they can and do say 'to God be the glory,' but they cannot say 'to God *alone* be the glory,' because they insist on mixing human power or ability with the human response to gospel grace."[114]

Accordingly, when free-will theists get to heaven, we will inevitably boast, "I chose to believe. I, by my own power, received Jesus Christ as my Savior."[115] Boice ends by suggesting that we fall into this error because we have not adequately grasped the weight of our human sinfulness.

All of this to say, free-will theism faces the charges of belittling human sinfulness, undermining salvation by grace, and stealing God's glory. Do the charges stick? What have we to say for ourselves? After sitting with these monsters for a while, here are some things I have come to say for myself.

Less of Sin?

Every human being has done something he did not think he was capable of. Sometimes that's good, but most of the time it's bad. You have a thought so repulsive that you are stunned it even entered your mind. You say something so cruel that you wonder how a human even thinks to say that to another human. You do something so selfish that you're left gazing into the mirror wondering, "Who am I, who does that?" It's a daily thing for me.

And yet I do not normally think of myself as some sort of hideously repulsive, cruel, and selfish creature. This leads me to believe that I (and probably every human who has ever existed) am unquestionably guilty of underestimating my own sinfulness—we are worse than we think we are. Truth is, as long as we're constantly surrounded by humans every bit as broken as we are, we'll never know the depths of our depravity—that will only come when we stand before our crucified Creator. But all that said,

I find that my free-will theism does not belittle my own sinfulness (any more than any theology does) so much as it magnifies God's grace.

It doesn't make less of sin—it just makes more of grace.

More of Grace

Calvinism attempts to stress sin and magnify grace by emphasizing our depravity: we are so depraved that God has to do every single bit of our salvation. God even determines our acceptance of the gift of salvation because we could not otherwise do so.

But as already noted, for me this undermined both sin and grace because God is the ultimate cause of our sinfulness and depravity and as such his saving us is not an act of grace—God is merely fixing the problem he caused. And so while I might respond to this gesture by saying, "God, you did the right thing," I certainly wouldn't respond by saying, "Thank you." Or at least I wouldn't know why I was saying, "Thank you." And as noted earlier, if you cannot stand before the cross and understand why you are saying, "Thank you," there's a big problem. Sin is no longer sin and grace is no longer grace. No, in order for sin to be sin and grace be grace, we must stress sin and magnify grace in another way. The other way is rather obvious once it is pointed out to you.

As copiously noted throughout, classic free-will theism wholeheartedly affirms totally depravity. Humans do not have the ability to turn to God on their own. We are black holes, hopelessly turned in on ourselves and are both guilty of and infected with sin. But it also affirms that *God's grace is more than capable of overcoming our depravity*. I mean seriously . . .

God's grace is capable of creating the cosmos, sustaining existence, and raising Jesus from the dead, but it can't overcome our depravity so as to give us the ability to accept or reject God's offer of redemption?[116] Instead of belittling sin and grace, I have come to believe free-will theism does the exact opposite.

The Contribution of Doing Nothing

But what about our ability to boast in our salvation? After all, we are the ones who "ultimately" decide whether we end up in heaven or hell. An illustration borrowed from Roger Olson might be helpful here.

A man has fallen into a pit, is unconscious, and will eventually die. But God calls out to the man and offers help, awakening him from his unconsciousness. God starts pouring water down into the pit and tells the man that if he will just stay still, he can float on the water up to rescue. All the man has to do is not struggle or try to hold on to the bottom. All he has to do to be saved is surrender.[117] His "contribution" to his salvation is the contribution of doing nothing.

Or by means of the classic analogy, salvation is a gift but a gift still has to be received. And what sort of idiot receives a gift and then starts boasting about how he used the muscles in his vocal chords, tongue, and mouth to say, "Yes, I will accept this gift"? He would be an idiot who is not fit for heaven to be sure, but then again none of us are.

But this is not enough for many Calvinists. After all, we are not just unconscious down in a pit but we are literally dead in our sins (Eph 2:1–9)! Fair enough—though I'm unsure what *literally* dead means—so let's just tweak Olson's analogy and say a dead man is down in a pit and God brings him back to life, and then gives him the option of allowing the water to float him up or fighting the water and securing his final death. That works for me. But isn't there still just a little smidgen of room for us to boast in our salvation, even if it's just 0.000000001 percent? And here we reach a stalemate. No, *I* don't think it leaves any of us any room to boast in our salvation—but a Calvinist does. We'll have to agree to disagree.

Thus while I understand the Calvinist concern, it simply doesn't seem to concern God as much as it concerns them.[118] I don't think a God who takes on flesh to be murdered by his creatures is too worried about being taken advantage of, so we probably need not worry ourselves to death with it either.

> No one need worry about our getting the best of God in some
> bargain with him . . . Anyone who thinks this is a problem has
> seriously underestimated the intelligence and agility of our Fa-
> ther . . . He will not be tricked or cheated. Any arrangement God

has established will be right for him and right for us. We can count on it.[119]

And to the extent that I can perceive such a thing, if I stand before the pearly gates and Saint Peter asks me why I was saved, I will say, "Because I was loved." Hopefully that'll do.

Foreknowledge and Evil

Another monster—or at least perplexing feature—of free-will theism regards God's foreknowledge.

According to classic theism, God has absolute, exhaustive foreknowledge of the future. According to a recent variation on classic theism called open theism, God does not have exhaustive foreknowledge of the future, but being infinitely intelligent, he certainly has a very good idea what is going to happen. Either way, this results in the following dilemma. If God knew—or at least had a very good idea (open theism)—that the world he was going to create would result in this much evil and the eternal damnation of an undisclosed number of humans, why would he create it? If God creates a world in which sin, evil, and hell are inevitable, is God not responsible for them and is the free-will theist not left in the same place as the Calvinist?

In the theological/philosophical world, it's a rare thing to see much of a consensus, but when it comes to this issue, there is remarkable agreement that it was put to bed by Alvin Plantiga's classic free-will defense:

> A world containing creatures who are significantly free (and freely perform more good than evil actions) is more valuable, all else being equal, than a world containing no free creatures at all. Now God can create free creatures, but He can't *cause* or *determine* them to do only what is right. For if He does so, then they aren't significantly free after all; they do not do what is right *freely*. To create creatures capable of *moral good*, therefore, He must create creatures capable of moral evil; and He can't give these creatures the freedom to perform evil and at the same time prevent them from doing so. As it turned out, sadly enough, some of the free creatures God created went wrong in the exercise of their freedom; this is the source of moral evil. The fact

that free creatures sometimes go wrong, however, counts neither against God's omnipotence nor against His goodness; for
He could have forestalled the occurrence of moral evil only by
removing the possibility of moral good.[120]

Notice that Plantiga has not stated that his conclusions are bulletproof. He
is merely pointing out that it is certainly possible that God chose to create
this world—knowing it would result in this much sin, evil, and suffering—because it was not possible for him to create a world in which great
moral good and genuine divine/human relationships were possible and
evil was not. You don't have to agree with it, but it's hard to disagree that
it's a possibility.

And in addition to hearing a possibility, those of us grounded in
the story of scripture hear echoes of Eden—God placing two trees before
Adam, giving him the option to live within or outside of God's design for
creation. Thus, while God did create a world in which he knew (or was
pretty sure) some of his creatures would end up in hell, he had no better
options if his creatures were to be genuinely free and capable of having
genuine relationships with him.

While this explanation is possible and—seems to me—biblical, it
must be admitted that it is still leaves one feeling a bit uncomfortable.
Yes, those in hell are there because of their own sinful thoughts, actions,
and inclinations. They deserve hell just like we all do. But God brought
these humans into existence knowing they would/could turn out like this,
knowing they would/could spend eternity in hell.[121] This can seem a high
price to pay and we are left capitulating to a mystery, trusting that God
knew what he was doing when he created this world and not another.

Bliks

Have you ever seen the duck rabbit?

It's an image of a duck . . . or a rabbit. Depending on how you look
at it, you either see a duck or a rabbit.[122] Both are there to be seen and it's
tough to say why some people initially see the duck and others see the
rabbit. This is a crude example of what philosophers call a blik. A blik is an
interpretive lens through which we see everything else. A blik is why some
see the glass half full, while others see it half empty. A blik is why some

look at suffering and see the absence of God, while others look at suffering and see the presence of God. We see the same thing through different eyes and thus see different things.

And in many ways, bliks are the reason why some people opt for Calvinism while others opt for free-will theism.[123] Calvinists read the Bible and what jumps out to them is God's all-determining sovereignty and commitment to glorify himself at all costs—*their blik is the glory of power.* Free-will theists read the Bible and what jumps out to them is the self-giving sovereignty of Jesus in which love is more important than con-trol—*their blik is the glory of love.*

Living Mysteries

And at the end of the day, I have no clue why one blik comes more natu-rally to us than the other. But I do think I have a clue why, having seen other options, we choose to stick with our blik or get a new one. When it comes down to it, I think we stick with a theological home because we prefer the monsters in its basement to the monsters in other basements. People don't choose Calvinism or free-will theism because one side has clearly proven itself right, but because they "find one set of mysteries easier to live with than the other."[124]

And so what mysteries are you willing to live with, to live out? Bet-ter yet, what mysteries do you think the Bible teaches you to live with? Perhaps the Apostle Paul gets nearest the heart of the supreme mystery:

> For I want you to know how great a struggle I have on your be-half . . . and for all those who have not personally seen my face, that their hearts may be encouraged, having been knit together in love, and attaining to all the wealth that comes from the full assurance of understanding, *resulting in a true knowledge of God's mystery, that is, Christ Himself,* in whom are hidden all the treasures of wisdom and knowledge. (Col 2:1–3)

The mystery is Jesus, God incarnate and God crucified *for the whole world.* As Maximus the Confessor said long ago, "It is the mystery of love and the mystery of freedom which is the mystery of God, three in one."[125]

As such, no matter what monsters I must learn to live with, I am going to live in a home that does what the Bible does: whirl round and round the mystery of Christ, the mystery of love.

9

Walking With a Limp

Crossing the Jabbok

Jacob wants to go home. He's been gone for a long time, on a long journey. "Return to the land of your fathers," God says; and Jacob agrees.[127] So he packs up camp and heads home, but there is trepidation in his steps. Jacob didn't exactly leave on the best terms. He deceived his father, stole a blessing from his brother, and was then sent away to live with relatives. What sort of reception will he receive? Is Esau still angry enough to kill him? It's tough to tell.

So Jacob does what he's done all along: he plans and he manipulates. He sends all his family and all his servants ahead to meet Esau first, to flatter him with compliments and to give him lots of goats, camels, cows, and donkeys. And now he stands alone at the edge of the Jabbok River. Dusk gives way to evening as the sun dips under the horizon. In the morning he will cross the Jabbok and be home—if he makes it through the night.

Suddenly—a rustling in the bushes.

Jacob sits up, his eyes strain to focus, but before they get a chance it happens. A stranger pounces from the dark and Jacob is fighting for his life. Who is it? Esau? An evil spirit guarding the river crossing? They wildly grapple, kicking up dust and grass, and all the while Jacob's eyes still strain to focus on his attacker's face but to no avail. The stranger remains a mystery.

The muscles burn and the adrenaline wears thin, but neither party will surrender. The stranger is strong but Jacob is resolved. Indeed, it appears Jacob may win! But then it all unravels with a simple touch. The stranger touches Jacob's hip, dislocating it, and instantly Jacob howls in agony as he falls to the ground. He lies there crippled and broken, and yet he has not let go of his attacker—Jacob has pulled him to the ground.

Covered in dirt and sweat, Jacob clutches him with white knuckles until he sees the first rays of sunlight beating back the night. The stranger sees it too and his tone is urgent when he says, "Let me go, for the dawn is breaking!" Then Jacob's eyes grow wide for he has finally gotten a peek of his attacker's face:

> What he sees is something more terrible than the face of death—
> the face of love. It is vast and strong, half ruined with suffering
> and fierce with joy, the face a man flees down all the darkness
> of his days until at last he cries out, "I will not let you go, unless
> you bless me!"[128]

Israel

The stranger then breaks his silence with a curious question: what is your name? "Jacob," he responds, refusing to lose his grip despite suspicions that the intruder he holds is something utterly Other. But Jacob's suspicions, grandiose as they are, cannot anticipate what comes next—he receives a new name: "Your name shall no longer be Jacob, but Israel, because you have struggled with God and with humans and overcome."[129] Bewildered, Jacob lets go and considers the impossible.

He has been fighting with God.

His hands have clutched the divine.

And now he has received a name that marks this brush with deity. Jacob is now Israel, and the nation that will spring forth from him is the nation born in this assault from God. Israel is the nation born at the moment when Jacob defeated God. Or did he?

The story ends with the sun rising on Jacob as he limps home: "Now the sun rose upon him just as he crossed over Penuel, and he was limping . . ."[130]

Cripples and Crumbs

This is what happens when humans encounter God.

Whether we call it a magnificent defeat or a crippling victory, when we bump up against the Mystery of mysteries, we receive a blessing but we also walk away with a limp.[131] When dealing with I AM, we are all cripples seeking crumbs. And perhaps the surest sign that our theology actually brushes against God is the presence of a limp. It is the cultivation of humility, candor, and generosity. It is a certain trepidation, modesty, and restraint. Theology that doesn't limp is not Christian theology.

When one surveys the current theological scene, there is lots of swaggering but little limping. It's a puzzling phenomenon. We're claiming to speak of and even for God, for the Creator and Sustainer of the cosmos. We're claiming to speak for the voice that spoke the universe into existence. We're claiming to describe the Mystery behind all other mysteries. And yet we swagger? Where does our swagger come from? The seeds of theological swagger usually germinate in the same place: certainty.

The Certainty Itch

From the moment Adam and Eve bit into the ill-fated piece of fruit, humans have tried to transcend transcendence. We reject our humanity and grasp for divinity. This grasping takes many different forms, but often shows itself in our audacious attempts to achieve certainty in our knowledge of God. Neither faith nor probability is enough. We want knowledge that cannot be doubted.

This is especially the case in the present theological and philosophical milieu in which many of us feel we are drowning in a sea of relativism, skepticism, and nihilism. Everything is doubted, no one has conviction, and we are desperate for a safe strip of dry land. This makes certainty and theological swagger all the more appealing: "Our appetite for certainty has only grown in our troubled century. The further away it is, the more desirable it seems."[132] We swarm like bugs to the light of swaggering theologians, movements, and institutions so we might be saved from the boogeyman of postmodernism (or post-postmodernism, or meta-modernism, or . . . whatever).

Descartes

But the great irony and tragedy in all of this is that much of the skepticism we now endure was precipitated by a similar attempt to achieve certainty in our knowledge of God.

It was seventeenth-century Europe, and atheism was crouching at the door. Worried it would soon kick down the doors of the church, Cardinal Pierre de Berulle enlisted the help of a promising young philosopher, Rene Descartes. Descartes was to prove, beyond doubt, the existence of God. To do so, he had to clear the ground of anything that was not certain; that is, he discarded as unreliable any sort of knowledge that he could doubt.[133]

The repercussions of this method on subsequent human thought and culture cannot be overstated, but for our purposes the most important is this. Indubitable, objective certainty became the only knowledge that really counted as knowledge: "The modern age began with the daring program of Descartes, a program encouraged by a cardinal of the church and designed to banish skepticism once and for all by establishing the method by which indubitable certainty could be obtained."[134] It sounded promising enough, but eventually it became clear that certainty is a seductress, a tease, and ultimately, an illusion.

Subsequent generations pointed out that if objective knowledge is the only sort that really counts, then no meaningful human knowledge is possible because there is no such thing as objective knowledge. Everyone "knows" from a perspective. Everything can be doubted. *Objective truth can only be known subjectively.* And if everything can be doubted and the only knowledge that counts is knowledge that can't be doubted, then we are in quite a predicament. We have backed ourselves into a blind alley. It's no wonder things have spiraled into a quagmire of skepticism and doubt.

Lament if you must, but the way out of our dilemma is simply not to beat the certainty drum louder and louder. Nor is it swaggering around, hoping our pomp will compensate for the ignorance and doubt we inevitably harbor as tiny piles of dust in the vast cosmos of our Creator. No, certainty and swagger will not save us from skepticism.

But limping will.

God is a Person

Central to Christian belief is the conviction that God is, in some sense, a person.[135] God is not an object to be examined or an equation to be solved. God is a person to be known, and reality, at its core, is personal. And if God is indeed a person—and an infinitely transcendent community of persons at that—then when it comes to our knowledge of God, certainty is impossible.[136]

Finite human beings are trying to know an infinite Person(s) as we stare at the universe through a pinhole. How could we possibly be certain or objective? What would that even mean? But before our anxiety cranks up too much, it must be noted that while our knowledge of God is not and can never be objective, neither is it wholly subjective. It is personal.

Who do you "know" best? Perhaps it's a spouse, friend, parent, or sibling. Now, what are some things you know about that person with absolute certainty, things that cannot be doubted? Maybe you're certain she is kind. You are with her everyday and watch her interactions with others. You've never heard her utter a cross word. But how could you ever be certain she was kind? Who knows what she does when you're not around? Perhaps she tortures kittens and puppies. And who knows everything that runs through her mind? Who knows what she would do if she could get away with it? You certainly don't know any of that, and so in the end all you can be certain about is that you experience her as kind. Her kindness can always be doubted.

And we can go round and round with scenario after scenario, but we will keep reaching this impasse—while you might be absolutely certain that you are certain in your knowledge of something, you most certainly are not certain. And that is because you always know as a person, as a being with a relentlessly limited perspective, and you can never transcend your "personhood" so as to achieve some sort of objectively certain knowledge. As Leslie Newbigin says, "It is obviously absurd to suppose that total objectivity is possible; for, if there is no subject who knows, there is no knowing."[137]

Personal Knowledge

And herein lies the way out of skepticism and relativism. We must embrace the fact that all of our knowing is, ultimately, personal. It is the knowledge we have as painfully finite persons. And even more so, the most meaningful type of knowledge we can have is knowledge of other persons. On both ends, genuine knowledge is personal:

> The implication is that all our knowing is personal, not only in the sense that it involves the personal and passionate commitment of the knower but also in the sense that our knowledge will not be complete unless it presses beyond impersonal realities (explored with the tools of physics, chemistry, biology and the human sciences) to that personal reality . . . [138]

This means that we must accept and embrace the risk involved in all human knowing, especially our knowing of God. We could most certainly be wrong and our most cherished beliefs can certainly be doubted. But this does not make our knowledge inadequate or less meaningful. Far from it! It just means that we must reject the naive notion that the most meaningful type of knowledge is knowledge that cannot be doubted.

Rather, the opposite is true: the most meaningful type of knowledge—personal knowledge—can always be doubted! It is the personal commitment of a person to another person. It is not a leap of blind faith but it is a step out onto uncertain ground. We can and should be confident—deeply confident—but we cannot be certain:

> Surely it *must* be an illusion to imagine that there can be available to us a kind of certainty that does *not* involve this personal commitment. This at least must surely be said: if the biblical depiction of the human situation is true; *if* the supreme reality is a personal God whose we are and to whom we are responsible; then there is something quite absurd about the posture of those who claim infallible certainty about God . . . In our interpersonal relations, we would never make such a claim . . . How absurd to make such a claim with respect to God! [139]

Good Manners = Good Theology

And this is why humility, restraint, and moderation in our beliefs about God are not simply good manners. *They are good theology.*

Far from being the marks of spinelessness or skepticism, they are the marks of a theology that limps because it is actually dealing, wrestling, and struggling with God. They are the marks of a theology that has stopped trying to transcend transcendence. They are the marks of a person who has quit the tired, doomed rebellion against finitude; the marks of a human who has embraced being a human—riskiness, uncertainty and all. We're humans and that means we don't get to be certain. And this is why one of the noblest, purest, and most Christian of theological confessions is the acknowledgement of our humanity instead of the concealment of it behind the flimsy charades of swagger and certainty.

It's not certainty or bust; faith always has room for doubt, and that's not such a bad thing. As Daniel Taylor says, "My own experience is that for human beings certainty does not exist, has never existed, will not—in our finite states—ever exist, and, moreover, should not. It is not a gift God has chosen to give His creatures, doubtlessly wisely."[140] Or as Buechner says, "Doubts are the ants in the pants of faith. They keep it awake and moving."[141] Rather than destroying faith, doubt and uncertainty can animate it by moving us towards that proper posture of humbled humanity and confident submission. We defang doubt when we stare it down and accept it *into* faith.

And that's why it may not be too much to say that doubt is closer to faith than certainty is. Doubt—if accepted as the inescapable thorn in the side of humanity—can give birth to faith when we bring it before the Christ who hung on the cross and said, *"My God, my God, why have you forsaken me?"*

Faith, doubt, humility, and confidence—this is the stuff and substance of theology at its best. Swagger, smugness, and certainty—this is the stuff and substance of ideology at its worst.

Speaking the Unspeakable

I have an opinion. I'm confident in my theology. I think Calvinists are right on some things, kind of wrong on some things, and really wrong on some things. I probably do my fair share of swaggering. And I've shared my journey because I think there's a better way and I'd like you to join me on it. But I could be wrong and I must be OK with that, because perhaps the only thing worse than being wrong is being certain you're right—a statement that is less about manners and tolerance than it is theology and honesty.

Barth once famously said, "We ought to speak of God. We are human, however, and so cannot speak of God. We ought therefore to recognize both our obligation and our inability and by that very recognition give God the glory. This is our perplexity. The rest of our task fades into insignificance in comparison."[142]

We cannot really speak of God.

We cannot stop speaking of God.

This is indeed our perplexity—mine and yours—and it's a perplexity that is never solved. It's only embraced. Confidence? Most definitely. Certainty? No. You're a human and I am too—that's a fact. So let's trade in our swagger for a limp and start looking for crumbs together.

10

Young, Restless, and . . .

Gospel Dilemma

So that's my pilgrimage in and out of Calvinism, my wanderings of deconstruction and reconstruction. And while a theological journey never comes to an end this side of the grave, we can find a home along the way—God knows we need one. I have one and I'm learning to limp around in it. I'm kind of young, I'm restless, and I'm . . .

Well, I'm still not quite sure how to finish that sentence. Young, restless, and Reformed just rolls off the tongue. Young, restless, and a free-will theist doesn't have the same ring to it. *And in addition to being a rhetorical dilemma, this is a gospel dilemma* because that sentence needs to end with something about the gospel. If the gospel is indeed the radiant hub of Christian faith, life, worship, and mission, then we would do well to center ourselves on it instead of becoming fixated on one of its spokes.

Regardless of your theological persuasion, the gospel is not primarily a proclamation of Calvinism or free-will theism (or any other "ism" for that matter); although you'd be excused for thinking it was, given the tenor of some people. Nor is the gospel "the good news that, because of Jesus' death alone, your sins can be forgiven, and all you have to do is believe it, rather than trying to impress God with doing 'good works.'"[143] No, as a growing avalanche of voices are pointing out, the gospel is something much bigger than justification by faith, double imputation, and substitutionary atonement.[144] As an evangelical Protestant, I think these doctrines have their place, but they are not the gospel. If we want to be people who live and speak the gospel, then we need to go to the Gospels (Matthew, Mark, Luke, and John . . . they're called the Gospels for a reason), and there we find that the key words in gospel vernacular are *kingdom, cross,* and *discipleship.*

Kingdom

In both Matthew 4:23 and 9:35, we are told that Jesus was "proclaiming the gospel of the kingdom." If we want to take our cue from Jesus—usually a bright idea—then perhaps we should at least attempt to define the gospel in kingdom terms. The gospel is a message about a king and kingdom. And as N. T. Wright, Scot McKnight, and a host of others have laboriously pointed out, the gospel is the good news that God has become king of the whole universe in and through the story of Jesus:

> A new state of affairs has been brought into existence. A door has been opened that nobody can shut. Jesus is now the world's rightful Lord, and all other lords are to fall at his feet.[145]

> Notice this: what God does in sending the Son is to establish Jesus as the Messiah, which means King, and God established in Jesus Christ the kingdom of God, which means the King is ruling in his kingdom. We need to restate this: the idea of King and a kingdom are connected to the original creation. God wanted . . . Adam and Eve to rule in this world. They failed, so God sent his Son to rule. As its King and Messiah and Lord, the Son commissions the Church to bear witness to the world of redemption in Jesus Christ, the true King, and to embody the kingdom as the people of God.[146]

This is the gospel.[147] The King and his kingdom have come crashing in, and all other kingdoms had better take notice and gratefully kneel in submission before the kneeling is no longer optional. And this is the invitation of the gospel: as Jesus said it, "Repent, for the kingdom of heaven is at hand."[148] Surrender your little fiefdom over to the only One who is truly sovereign.

And when you take a closer look at the gospel of the kingdom, you'll find that instead of reigning from some celestial throne up in the heavens, the God of the gospel reigns from a cross.

Cross

In Mark 10, James and John ask Jesus a question: "Can we sit on your right and left when you come in your glory?" That is, "Can we have the best seats when you are crowned king and lead out the heavenly army, establishing the kingdom of God and trampling everyone and everything else?"

A fair request, to be sure, and so Jesus responds, "You don't know what you're asking for. First off, those seats have already been assigned, and more importantly, I don't think you would want them anyways. You see, you think I am going to do things the way you would do things. You think I'm going to trample my enemies and respond to violence with more violence and make sure nobody gets the best of me. But I'm not like you and my kingdom is not like any you've ever seen. And if you want a place in my kingdom, then you've got to give your life away. For even I, the King, did not come to be served but to serve and give my life away as a ransom for many."[149]

Jump ahead to Mark 15. The disciples have scattered, and Jesus hangs on the cross alone. Only he's not alone, as we are told that two criminals are crucified with him . . . one on his right and one on his left. This of course reminds us of the conversation Jesus had with James and John, in which they asked if they could sit on his right and left when he came in his glory, when he became king. And here we see the stunning paradox of the crucifixion: Jesus's crucifixion is the moment when Jesus is enthroned as king, the moment when he comes in his glory, the moment the universe has anxiously awaited but could have never anticipated.[150]

And so God's epic plan to set everything right, to deal with sin, to judge the world, to establish his kingdom on earth as it is in heaven, reaches its climax on the cross as God takes all the hurt and hate and violence and sin upon himself and . . . forgives it. He puts sin and death to death by smothering it with suffering, self-giving love. Love has had the last word, and now everything can be redeemed. The gospel of the kingdom is the gospel of the cross-shaped kingdom of the crucified King of the universe:

> We have, alas, belittled the cross, imagining it merely as a mechanism for getting us off the hook of our own petty naughtiness . . . It is much, much more. It is the moment when the story of Israel reaches its climax; the moment when, at last, the watchmen on Jerusalem's walls see their God coming in his kingdom; the moment when the people of God are renewed so as to be, at last, the royal priesthood who will take over the world not with the love of power but with the power of love; the moment when the kingdom of God overcomes the kingdoms of the world. It is the moment when a great old door, locked and barred since our first disobedience, swings open . . . [151]

And so for those with the stomach for it, how do we enter the cross-shaped kingdom of the crucified God?

Discipleship

Follow me.

Search the Gospels far and wide, and you'll find this is the only invitation Jesus ever really extends to anyone. As Dallas Willard notes, the New Testament is a book by disciples, about disciples, for disciples.[152] The kingdom is for disciples: people who are learning to follow Jesus in the entirety of their life so they might be transformed in the entirety of their being; people who are following Jesus so they can become like him.[153] You cannot opt in to Christianity but out of discipleship. Disciples aren't super Christians; they're just Christians.

And bundled up in this word "disciple" is a cluster of other important ideas: trusting in Jesus, asking him "into your heart," having your sins forgiven. And while these things are important, they can never be taken as an invitation to something other than discipleship. It's discipleship or bust. Discipleship is the entrance to the kingdom.

Jesus's intention—and the intention of the gospel—was and is to create a community of disciples that loves God with heart, mind, soul, and strength and loves its neighbors as itself. It was to create a community where the crucified King reigns. Nothing else will do because this is what the gospel does: it makes disciples of the cross-shaped kingdom of the crucified God and King, Jesus.

Disciples: Manufactured or Organic?

As mentioned earlier, it is often said that one's theology is not tenable unless it can be preached at the gates of Auschwitz. It would seem the gospel forces us to also say that one's theology is not tenable unless it naturally produces disciples of the kingdom.

If you have a pulse and a decent set of eyes, then you know that "non-discipleship is the elephant in the church."[154] Evangelicalism is littered with pseudo-gospels and theologies that produce consumers of religious goods and services instead of disciples. Both Calvinism and free-will theism, in their various forms and expressions, are no exception. But once it has been conceded that everyone's hands are a little dirty, there's a question that begs asking. Do Calvinism or free-will theism *naturally* produce disciples of the kingdom?

The question is painfully slippery because (as mentioned above) there are so many variations and expressions of each. That said and conceded, I still think it's a question worth considering.

Will That Matters

I know many Calvinists who are radiant disciples of the kingdom. I have seen Neo-Calvinism challenge scores of my own friends and congregants to pick up their crosses and follow Jesus. I myself first started taking discipleship seriously when I was young, restless, and Reformed. But the question is not whether or not Calvinism—and Neo-Calvinism in particular—is producing disciples. It obviously can and does.

The question is whether the emphases of Calvinism *naturally* produce disciples. And from my finite perspective and limping experience, they do not—at least according to the understanding of discipleship I've sketched above. Neo-Calvinism can and does manufacture disciples; I just don't know that it can grow them organically. And what it really comes down to is this.

At the heart of gospel-driven discipleship, there is the decision, by grace through faith, to surrender self and follow Jesus—that is, at the heart of gospel-driven discipleship, there is the belief that you have a choice and therefore a will that matters.

In the human mind, choice is deeply tied to meaning, so much so that we don't know how to find meaning without choice. My wife finds meaning in me sending her a bouquet of roses because she knows I could have chosen not to. If someone put a gun to my head and made me send her a bouquet, the roses have lost meaning because I had no choice. We find meaning in Jesus dying for us because we believe he did not have to. If Jesus had no choice, I'm not sure what we would find in the cross, but I don't think we would find any meaning in it. It didn't *mean* anything—it just happened.

And far from being some human evolutionary construct invented to add significance to our existence, I believe Jesus shows this connection between choice and meaning lies at the heart of the gospel—of kingdom, cross, and discipleship. Daily Jesus challenges you to follow him up on the cross so your old self can continue to be crucified, and daily you must decide if you will do so. Daily Jesus invites you to join him on mission, reaching out to the lost and the least, and daily you must decide if you will do so. "What will you, by the grace of God, do with your will?"—Jesus asks us again and again.

Exercises in Chasing Your Tail

And in Calvinism, you simply do not have a choice and therefore do not have a will that matters. So the questions, "What will you do with your will? What will you do with your kingdom?" are rendered unintelligible.

You may have the illusion of a will that matters, but if you pull back the curtain, God's will is the only game in town. Regardless of the passion of the rhetoric you crank out to make sense of it, the fact is that God has already decided whether or not you will follow Jesus, share the gospel, deny yourself, and surrender your kingdom. Your will does not matter—at least not in any sense that we can make sense of.

And yet you are expected to act as though it does. You're supposed to run on the treadmill and pretend you're running the race of faith. This forces you into the awkward position of seemingly *suspending your theology in order to live faithfully*—because living faithfully requires living with meaning and living with meaning requires choice. You believe God determines all things, and yet act as though your will is not completely determined.

To be clear, I'm not saying Calvinism can't produce faithful disciples (again, it can and does). I'm just saying that in order to do so, it must talk and think about our wills as if they matter (have a choice) even though its theological underpinnings have already made it clear they do not. Plenty of people nevertheless do it, but it makes me dizzy—like a dog chasing his tail. And in the end, I don't know that this sort of cognitive dissonance and mental gymnastics organically produces disciples of the kingdom.

Young, Restless, Following Jesus

So how about free-will theism? Does it naturally produce disciples? I'm going to hedge a bit and rephrase that question: can it naturally produce disciples? Yes, I think it can. Because despite its many flaws, at the heart of free-will theism there is the belief that, by the grace of God, we have a choice and therefore a will that matters—the same belief that lies at the heart of gospel-driven discipleship.

So not only does discipleship fit into the narrative of free-will theism; it seems to be the thread that holds it all together. From being created in the imago Dei, to the trees in the garden, to the tree upon which the crucified God of self-giving love was hung, to the tree of life in the resurrected kingdom of God, we are invited to submit our rule to God's by following Jesus in discipleship, and reign with him "forever and ever." There is a deeply organic relationship here. Free-will theism provides discipleship a fitting home.

And perhaps that's the best way to end that sentence. I'm kind of young, I'm still restless, and I'm learning to follow Jesus.

11

Taming the Tiger (A.K.A. Romans 9)

Romans 9, Again

In order to end my story, it seems inevitable that we should end back up at Romans 9—that roaring tiger that devoured John Piper's free-will theism and did the same with mine. I understand if you still think it is licking its chops, eager to devour everything I've said so far. I would disagree with you, but I can understand.

This chapter is called "Taming the Tiger," but that's a bit misleading because I don't care much about taming Romans 9—I care about unleashing it. Because make no mistake, Romans 9 is one gnarly, aggressive text; however, it's aggressiveness is rooted in its mercy, not its narrowness. Romans 9 has teeth, but they're for saving, not damning.

I'm no Pauline scholar, but I do know how to read people who are, so I'd like to conclude by offering a few thoughts by way of summary, highlighting what many biblical scholars believe Romans 9—or better yet 9–11—teach.

What About Israel?

First off, we have context—something that demands a confession of sorts on the part of evangelical Bible readers. Never is bad evangelical Bible reading—characterized most by our aversion to particularity,

chronological snobbery, and egoism—more on display than in Paul's letter to the Romans.

In other words, if you mistakenly read the Bible as if it were a collection of books, letters, oracles, and poems written *to you* (answering all
your questions, addressing all your concerns) instead of its actual recipi-
ents (be they post-exilic Jews, first-century Jewish Christians, or puzzled
Roman Gentiles), Romans is going to expose you and expose you quickly.
As N. T. Wright notes, "For too long we have read Scripture with nine-
teenth-century eyes and sixteenth-century questions. It's time to get back
to reading with first-century eyes and twenty-first-century questions."[155]

So what do we see when we read Romans 9–11, as best we can,
through first-century eyes? What issues is *Paul* dealing with?

The first thing we see—and blindingly so—is that this is not a theological aside, meant to clear up the determinism/free-will dilemma. It's
not as if Paul's scribe, noticing an indecisive pause in his dictation, suggests Paul lecture a bit on the finer points of Calvinism before moving on
to some specific instructions for the Roman community. As Paul himself
might say, "By no means!"

Rather, all that Paul has said up until this point—about the impar-
tiality of God, about the people of God being Jew and Gentile united
in Christ, about the inadequacy and obsoleteness of the Law, about all
coming to God on the basis of grace and faith in Jesus the Messiah—has
begged the question of Israel. Why has Israel, by and large, rejected its Messiah? What is God doing with Israel? Has he forsaken his first chosen
people (Israel) for a new chosen people (Gentiles)? If so, hasn't God been
unfaithful to his promises to Israel?

As Romans 9:1–6 make clear, these questions are the glasses through
which we must read chapters 9–11 and if you take them off for a second,
everything is going to get fuzzy.

Paul, Jews, and Rome

Now I know, I know: none of those questions really concern us.

We don't care about what God was up to with Israel and we certainly
don't lose sleep pondering his apparent lack of faithfulness to the covenant
he made with Abraham. So we assume (see how it works?) that because
we don't care about those things, Paul doesn't either because Paul wrote

Romans to us. But Paul is not writing to us, and apathetic to the questions as we may be, Paul cares about them and cares about them deeply, and woe to us if we attempt to whitewash and de-Judaize Romans 9–11 so it's easier for us to handle and "apply to our lives."

As a Jewish follower of Jesus, the Israel question left Paul in great angst in general (9:2–3), but was especially pertinent to the situation in Rome. We know that Rome had a history of anti-Judaism and that Jews were kicked out of Rome in the late 40s, so it seems likely (and chapter 11 confirms) that Roman Gentiles were predisposed to look down on Jews.[156] They were an inferior race that had overwhelmingly rejected the Jesus you worshiped. It's a volatile combination, sure to produce confusion and hubris on the part of the Gentile Christians in Rome.

Paul then writes as a *Jewish* Christian, trying to explain how Israel's rejection of its Messiah does not mean God has forsaken Israel, nor does it leave any room for Gentile arrogance. Ben Witherington puts it succinctly:

> Paul must rebut the notions that God has forsaken his first chosen people, that the Word of God has failed, and that Israel has stumbled so as to be permanently lost. Underlying these rebuttals is the refutation of the assumption of Gentile superiority in the Roman church. Here as elsewhere Paul is seeking to level the playing field so as to make clear that all are "in" the people of God by God's mercy and grace and that no one has a right to boast in his or her own accomplishments. He also wants to make clear that the salvation of Israel is still part of God's game-plan . . .[157]

With this context firmly in view, we can now read the rest of Romans 9–11 and avoid missing the forest for the trees.

Hardening and Mercy

So what is going on with Israel?

Appropriately enough, Paul answers this question by retelling Israel's history, illustrating that from start to finish the faithfulness and mercy of God have been stronger than the faithlessness of Israel.[158] From the patriarchs (9:6–13), to the exodus (9:14–18), to the exile (9:19–29), God has found a way to overcome the futility of Israel's sin and circumstances so he might show the riches of his glory upon vessels of mercy, both Jew and Gentile (9:23–24). God wants a massive, worldwide family of redeemed sinners and he's going to get it. Israel was supposed to help make that happen by their obedience, but because they have failed, God will nevertheless make it happen by their disobedience.

In terms of the exodus, God does not cause Pharaoh's sinfulness (Pharaoh had already enslaved God's people—Exodus 1:8–14), but hardens Pharaoh in his pre-existing sinfulness so God's name and power might be proclaimed throughout the whole earth. In the same way, God does not cause Israel's sin, but has "partially hardened" them in their pre-existing sin so the "fullness of Gentiles" can come in (11:25). It is simply bad Bible reading to ignore the parallel in Pharaoh and Israel's hardening, failing to acknowledge that if Israel's hardening is not a decree of reprobation (as 11:11–32 make clear), neither is Pharaoh's. Now, as in the past, God uses—and not causes—human faithlessness to enlarge his family. Paul offers a nice summary in 9:30–32:

> What shall we say then? That Gentiles, who did not pursue righteousness, attained righteousness, even the righteousness which is by faith; but Israel, pursuing a law of righteousness, did not arrive at that law. Why? Because they did not pursue it by faith, but as though it were by works.

In no uncertain terms, Paul says that Israel has stumbled and rejected their Messiah *because they failed to pursue righteousness by faith.* They did not stumble because God unilaterally hardened them, but because they pursued righteousness "as though it were by works" (9:32). Conversely, the Gentiles have attained righteousness, not because God unilaterally chose to save them, but because they pursued it by faith. In other words, *Paul explains mercy and hardening as God's response to faith and unbelief,* not unilateral, eternal decisions to save or damn individuals. And lest we miss the point, Paul clarifies this at least two more times. In 11:20–21, he says:

> Quite right, they [the Jews] were broken off for their unbelief, but you stand by your faith. Do not be conceited, but fear; for if God did not spare the natural branches [Israel], He will not spare you [Gentiles], either. Behold then the kindness and severity of God; to those who fell, severity, but to you, God's kindness,

> if you continue in His kindness; otherwise you also will be cut
> off. And they [Israel] also, if they do not continue in their un-
> belief, will be grafted in, for God is able to graft them in again.

Using the image of an olive tree, Paul says that the Jews have been broken
off *for their unbelief* whereas the Gentiles have been grafted in *because of
their faith*. And again we come around to 11:25:

> For I do not want you, brethren, to be uninformed of this mys-
> tery—so that you will not be wise in your own estimation—that
> a partial hardening has happened to Israel until the fullness of
> the Gentiles has come in . . .

Partial Hardening

This is what has happened to Israel. Because they have rejected their Messiah, God has hardened Israel in order to open wide the kingdom to the
Gentiles. God has used Israel's unbelief as an opportunity to blow the
doors of the kingdom off its hinges. *But this is a partial, temporary hardening.* It is no foreordained, unconditional decree of damnation. Israel
has indeed been hardened and cut off, but they can be grafted back in if
they will not continue in their unbelief (11:23). Paul Achtemeier helpfully
notes:

> The difficulty lies in the fact that those who have understood
> these verses to be statements of eternal truth about how God
> deals with each individual, rather than a statement of how God
> has dealt with Israel in pursuing his plan for the redemption of
> a rebellious creation . . . He is making a statement about how
> God dealt with Israel, and continues to deal with it, even when it
> rejects his Son; namely, with it in mercy, even when it deserves
> wrath . . . The passage is therefore about the enlargement of
> God's mercy to include Gentiles, not about the narrow and pre-
> determined fate of each individual.[159]

In the end, Paul puts a bow on the whole conversation: "For God has
shut up all in disobedience so that He may show mercy to all" (11:32). As
Witherington says:

> This means that all Paul has said about hardening and Israel being vessels of wrath was a *temporary* condition and had the ultimate purpose of God having mercy on all . . . God did this so all would have to relate to him on the basis of grace and faith, so none would think they had God in their debt, or that he owed them something.[160]

A Wideness in God's Mercy

All that has been said comes down to this.

The peculiar, winding, unorthodox plan of God, through Israel and for the world, is to shut up all in disobedience *so that he may show mercy to all.* The emphasis—from start to finish—is on God's desire to let people in, not keep people out. It is about the wideness of God's mercy, not its narrowness. Israel doesn't deserve it; the Gentiles don't deserve it, but God nevertheless gives it.

Far from being a treatise meant to justify God's righteousness in unconditional election, Romans 9–11 is a treatise about the incomprehensible mercy and scandalous faithfulness of God towards his creatures, through the crucified and resurrected Jesus Christ. Israel rejected their Messiah, but instead of rejecting Israel, God used their rejection to show mercy to the Gentiles. And in the end, God's desire is that he might show mercy to the whole world (11:32). The God of Romans 9–11 finds ways to show mercy, even when the facts clamor for judgment. This doesn't sound much like Calvinism to me, but it does sound a whole lot like Jesus.

Again, offering a verse-by-verse exposition of Romans 9–11 is above my pay grade—and has already been done many times—but these are some orienting thoughts that I have found helpful. Using the lens of the Israel question (9:1–6) and the interpretive vistas of 9:30–32 and 11:20–32 (as opposed to standing on top of 9:14–23 and interpreting the rest of the Bible from there), we catch a glimpse of a grander vision. I'd encourage you to read it now and see for yourself. For a more in-depth analysis from people with the credentials to do so, see any of the following works.

—William Klein, *The New Chosen People* (Grand Rapids: Zondervan, 1990).

—Ben Witherington III and Darla Hyatt, *Paul's Commentary to the Romans: A Socio-Rhetorical Commentary* (Grand Rapids: Eerdmans, 2004).

—N. T. Wright, "Romans," in *The New Interpreter's Bible*, Volume 10 (Nashville: Abingdon, 1994).

Epilogue
Lights Out

Switzerland?

I have a friend who, through a perplexing mix of nature and nurture, claims deep allegiances to both the University of Texas and Texas A&M University. He drives the rest of us crazy with his conflicting loyalties. I mean, you can't go to a Longhorns vs. Aggies football game and cheer for both—it just isn't right. Quit straddling that fence or you're going to hurt yourself. Nevertheless, he happily cheers along. It frustrates me, but I have to admit: he's the only person at the game who gets along with everyone (or thinks he does). In a sea of burnt orange and maroon, he's Switzerland.

Any time I come to the end of a particularly contentious debate, the first question that comes to my mind isn't, "Did I win?" but "Was it worth it?" Did I have to pick a side? Can we be neutral about this? Can we say *yes* to both? Is Switzerland a better option?

When it comes to free-will and Calvinism, the arguments can become so complex, the biblical evidence so open, and the debates so rabid that you can't help but wonder if the whole thing should be marked out as a theological Switzerland. Yes, God is infinitely good, and yes, God creates people to damn them. Yes, God looks like Jesus, and yes, God doesn't *completely* look like Jesus. Yes, we have real free will, and yes, God is the ultimate cause of every event.

In fact, be it a calculated choice or an unexamined contradiction, I think most people land in Switzerland on this issue. Those who lean towards free-will theism use Calvinism as a crutch when they want security and comfort. Those who lean towards Calvinism use free will as a crutch in order to perceive their lives, choices, and relationships—that is, their existence—as meaningful.

Jump!

And to those I would say, I like theological Switzerlands a lot more than I do theological Nazis—and you are most certainly free to land wherever you want—but does Switzerland really exist in this case or do you just wish it did? You *can* believe God unilaterally controls every single particle of reality and yet God doesn't control every single particle of reality, just like you *can* believe God created the world and didn't create the world (I suppose). No one can make you make sense—you *can* believe whatever you want.

But *why* believe something that, as far as we can tell, isn't a paradox but an outright contradiction?

Either God is the all-determining reality or he isn't (by his own choosing of course). I wish there were middle ground, but . . . where would it be? Nevertheless, maybe you still think it's the best option—maybe it is (that's the Swiss in me talking). But if nothing else, I hope what has preceded has shown there is another way; a way to have a sovereign, glorious God who still looks and loves like Jesus. While far from perfect, free-will theism has the gravitas to hold sovereignty, glory, grace, and love together. So sit on the fence as long as you want, but don't be afraid to jump.

Lights Out

Because one day the lights will go out.

That flickering flame of existence-as-we-know-it will be snuffed out by the grave. What will happen there, on the other side of death? It's a question riddled with intrigue and fear. We hear whispers of hope so profound they make the heart flutter. We catch glimpses of resurrection.

I don't know the timeline or mechanics of how it all works, but I wouldn't be too surprised if death sends us on a journey to the center of the universe. And what will we find there? Who will we find there?

Infinite inward energy or infinite outward energy?

An infinite inward collapse on Self or an infinite giving away of Self?

A Being who glorifies himself at all costs or loves at all costs?

A black hole or a mangled Lamb?

At the center of the universe, I think there's a Creator with holes in his hands, drenching the cosmos in a gratuitous downpour of love. He doesn't have to—he just wants to. It's who he is. And when the lights go out, the real show begins.

Endnotes

1. See footnote in the Introduction for explanation of my usage of the term "Neo-Calvinism."

2. John Piper, "Why God is Not a Megalomaniac in Demanding to Be Worshipped," accessed July 30th, 2012, www.desiringgod.org/resource-library/conference-messages/why-god-is-not-a-megalomaniac-in-demanding-to-be-worshiped.

3. John Piper, *The Pleasures of God: Meditations on God's Delight in Being God* (Sisters, OR: Multnomah, 2000), 11.

4. For more on Christian hedonism, read John Piper, *The Dangerous Duty of Delight* (Sisters, OR: Multnomah, 2001).

5. Eph 1:5–6, Ps 19:1, Isa 43:25, 48:11, 49:3, Jer 13:11, John 12:27–28, Hab 2:14, Rev 21:23.

6. John 3:16, 1 John 4:7–8.

7. Isa 55:8–9.

8. Frederick Buechner, *Wishful Thinking* (New York: HarperCollins, 1993), 112.

9. Rom 9:20.

10. For a wonderful explanation of this see Mark Talbot, "All the Good That Is Ours in Christ," in *Suffering and the Sovereignty of God*, eds. John Piper and Justin Taylor (Wheaton, IL: Crossway, 2006), 31–77.

11. And I know it's not that simple, but it's a good starting point.

12. John Piper, "An Interview with John Piper," eds. Piper and Taylor, *Suffering and the Sovereignty of God*, 220–21.

13. I am using *Reformed* and *Calvinism* synonymously here and they are not necessarily so. In fact, I know it will cause some great consternation that I have done so in this book. I ask for forgiveness. It's primarily a rhetorical decision as the terms have become synonymous in current American evangelicalism. As an evangelical Protestant, I consider myself Reformed in a certain sense, but recognize the term is now loaded with Calvinist theological presuppositions.

14. If you're interested, read Fulvio Melia's *The Black Hole at the Center of Our Galaxy* (Princeton, NJ: Princeton University Press, 2003).

15. 1 Tim 2:4, 2 Pet 3:9.

16. For the record, I love my mother-in-law.

17. Rev 20:11–15, Jude 1:3–13, Matt 25:31–46.

18. See Gregory McDonald, *The Evangelical Universalist,* 2nd ed. (Eugene, OR: Cascade, 2012).

19. Jonathan Edwards, *The End for Which God Created the World*, quoted by John Piper, *God's Passion for His Glory* (Wheaton, IL: Crossway, 2006), 151.

20. Well, maybe there will be, but not just because we want them there.

21. Anne Lamott (quoting her friend Tom), *Bird by Bird: Some Instructions on Writing and Life* (New York: Anchor, 1995), 21.

22. If you don't know what the DeLorean is, drop this book and go watch *Back to the Future*.

23. Jonathan Edwards, quoted by John Piper in "Is God Less Glorious Because He Ordained That Evil Be?," accessed June 20th, 2012, www.desiringgod.org/resource-library/conference-messages/is-god-less-glorious-because-he-ordained-that-evil-be.

24. Stephen Saint, "Sovereignty, Suffering, and the Work of Missions," eds. Piper and Taylor, *Suffering and the Sovereignty of God*, 118.

25. Ibid., 120.

26. There are lots of linguistic gymnastics used to explain the nature of God's ordaining the damnation of the reprobate. Some Calvinists would prefer to say God merely "passes over" the reprobate—he does not actively choose their damnation. But this is a distinction with no difference, a euphemism. Regardless of how it is couched, Calvinism must affirm that every single person in hell is there because God rendered it certain they would be.

27. John Calvin, *Institutes of the Christian Religion*, Library of Christian Classics vols. 20–21, ed. John T. McNeill, trans. Ford Lewis Battles (Philadelphia: Westminster, 1959), 3.24.17 (985). Jonathan Edwards, "Concerning the Divine Decrees in General and Election in Particular'" in ed. Edward Hickman, *The Works of Jonathan Edwards Volume II*, (Carlisle, PN: Banner of Truth Trust, 1974), 525–43. Piper, *The Pleasures of God*, 313–40. For a great discussion on how Calvinism logically necessitates double predestination see Roger Olson, *Against Calvinism* (Grand Rapids: Zondervan, 2011), 104–5.

28. Rev 21:4.

29. Or in philosophical terms, God's goodness must not be univocal, but neither can it be equivocal. It must be analogical.

30. Piper, *The Pleasures of God*, 336–37.

31. For just a few out of hundreds of examples, see Exod 22:21–27, Zech 7:8–14, Amos 2:6–8, Isa 58:5–10, Luke 16:19–31.

32. C. S. Lewis, *A Grief Observed* (New York: HarperCollins, 1994), 6–7.

33. J. K. Rowling, *Harry Potter and the Sorcerer's Stone* (New York: Scholastic Inc., 1997), 291.

34. Piper, *The Pleasures of God*, 146.

35. Leslie Newbigin, *Proper Confidence* (Grand Rapids: Eerdmans, 1995), 54–55.

36. David Baggett and Jerry Walls, *Good God: The Theistic Foundations of Morality* (New York: Oxford University Press, 2011), 78.

37. Here is a formal articulation of the problem, found on ibid., 245:

> 1) If we're not justified to believe the Bible was inspired by a morally perfect God, then we're not justified to think it's reliable.
>
> 2) If we're not justified to believe God is morally perfect, then we're not justified to believe the Bible was inspired by a morally perfect God.
>
> 3) If God is not recognizably good, then we're not justified to believe God is morally perfect.
>
> 4) If we're rational to believe that God damns those he could have saved without violating their free will, then God is not recognizably good.
>
> 5) If it is rational to believe Calvinism, then we're rational to believe God damns those he could have saved without violating their free will.

6) If it is rational to believe Calvinism, then God is not recognizably good.

7) If it is rational to believe Calvinism, then we're not justified to believe God is morally perfect.

8) If it is rational to believe Calvinism, then we're not justified to believe the Bible was inspired by a morally perfect God.

9) If it is rational to believe Calvinism, then we're not justified to think the Bible is reliable.

10) We are justified to believe the Bible is reliable.

11) Therefore, it is not rational to believe Calvinism.

38. I'm not claiming that Calvinists don't know what to do with the Bible or don't believe in its inspiration and authority. I am saying that as I tried to be a consistent Calvinist, I could no longer see any grounds for my belief in the inspiration and authority of scripture.

39. John Wesley, quoted by Roger Olson, *Arminian Theology: Myths and Realities* (Downer's Grove, IL: InterVarsity, 2006), 110.

40. See Roger Olson, *The Story of Christian Theology* (Downers Grove, IL: InterVarsity, 1999), 376.

41. Lewis, *A Grief Observed*, 31–32.

42. This is a story I found in Daniel Taylor's *The Skeptical Believer: Telling Stories to Your Inner Atheist* (Saint Paul, MN: Bog Walk Press, 2013), 27–28.

43. I would also note that theology is not an option. We all have a theological home. As C. S. Lewis says, if you think you don't "do" theology "that will not mean that you have no ideas about God. It will mean that you have a lot of wrong ones—bad, muddled, out-of-date ideas." *Mere Christianity* (New York: HarperCollins, 2001), 155.

44. N. T. Wright, *How God Became King: The Forgotten Story of the Gospels* (New York: HarperOne, 2011), 253–54.

45. Parker Palmer, *A Hidden Wholeness: The Journey Toward an Undivided Life* (San Francisco: Jossey-Bass, 2004), 36–37.

46. Brennan Manning, *Ruthless Trust: The Ragamuffin's Path to God* (New York: HarperCollins, 2000), 88.

47. Bruce Ware, *God's Greater Glory: The Exalted God of Scripture and the Christian Faith* (Wheaton, IL: Crossway, 2004), 41.

48. Ibid.

49. Leon Morris, "Hebrews," ed. Frank E. Gaebelein, *The Expositor's Bible Commentary*, vol. 12 (Grand Rapids: Zondervan, 1981), 14.

50. For a good discussion of this see Roger Olson, *The Story of Christian Theology*, 387–89.

51. B. A. Gerrish, "'To the Unknown God': Luther and Calvin on the Hiddenness of God," *Journal of Religion* 53 (1973), 276.

52. Many try to avoid this idea of the hidden God by speaking of God having "two wills" instead. But again, it's a distinction with no difference. Hidden God . . . two wills in God . . . they both add up to a schizophrenic God.

53. Dallas Willard, *The Divine Conspiracy: Rediscovering Our Hidden Life in God* (New York: HarperCollins, 1997), 334.

54. Mark Driscoll, "7 Big Questions." *Relevant Magazine*, Issue 24, August 2007. http://www.relevantmagazine.com/god/church/features/1344-from-the-mag-7-big-questions.

55. J. B. Phillips, *Your God Is Too Small* (New York: Touchstone, 2004), 27, 29.

56. Driscoll, "7 Big Questions."

57. John 2:4, Matt 12:46–50, 8:21–22, Luke 12:41–48, 14:16–24.

58. Rev 20:12.

59. Jürgen Moltmann, *The Crucified God* (Minneapolis: Fortress, 1993), 212.

60. Ibid., x.

61. Gregory Boyd, *Is God to Blame? Beyond Pat Answers to the Problem of Suffering* (Downers Grove, IL: InterVarsity, 2003), 35.

62. I once heard Brian McLaren pose this question.

63. Moltmann, *The Crucified God*, 205.

64. Luke 23:34.

65. Of course Calvinists are divided as to whether Christ died for the whole world or only the elect.

66. Boyd, *Is God to Blame?*, 52–53.

67. Piper, *The Pleasures of God*, 140.

68. Gerald Bray, *Romans,* ed. Gerald Bray, Ancient Christian Commentary on Scripture, New Testament vol. 6 (Downer's Grove, IL: InterVarsity, 1998), 244. Similarly, Gregory Boyd notes that no one prior to Augustine—except the dualistic and deterministic Manicheans—read Romans 9 in this fashion. Interestingly enough, Augustine was a Manichean prior to becoming a Christian. See Boyd, *Is God to Blame?*, 205.

69. Ibid., see in particular pages 250–64.

70. The Barmen Declaration, of which Barth was the primary author.

71. Joseph L. Mangina, *Karl Barth: Theologian of Christian Witness* (Louisville: Westminster John Knox, 2004), 3, cites this phrase and attributes it to Karl Adam in a Roman Catholic Monthly named *Das Hochland*, June 1926, 276–77.

72. Karl Barth, "Evangelical Theology in the 19th Century," in *The Humanity of God* (Richmond, VA: John Knox, 1960), 14.

73. Karl Barth, *Church Dogmatics* 2.1, ed. G.W. Bromiley and T.F. Torrance (Edinburgh: T & T Clark, 1957), 261.

74. Ibid., 273–74.

75. Ibid., 275.

76. Richard Hays, *The Moral Vision of the New Testament: A Contemporary Introduction to New Testament Ethics* (New York: HarperCollins, 1996), 202.

77. Ibid.

78. Barth, *Church Dogmatics*, 2.1, 276.

79. Ibid.

80. Ibid., 278.

81. Moltmann, *The Crucified God*, 214.

82. Barth, *Church Dogmatics*, 2.1, 279.

83. Miroslav Volf, *Free of Charge: Giving and Forgiving in a Culture Stripped of Grace* (Grand Rapids: Zondervan, 2005), 39.

84. Ibid., 64.

85. Barth, *Church Dogmatics*, 2.1, 301.

86. Ibid., 283–84.

87. For a brief discussion on the difference in libertarian and compatibilist free will see Chapter 8.

88. Ware, *God's Greater Glory*, 66–67.

89. Yes, sixty-three is a rough guess.

90. Although some scholars think it has a temporal meaning: "When God created

. . . "

91. Walter Brueggemann, *Genesis*, Interpretation (Atlanta: John Knox, 1982), 32.

92. See Nahum Sarna, *Genesis*, JPS Torah Commentary (Philadelphia: Jewish Publication Society, 1989), 12.

93. Terence Fretheim, "Genesis," *The New Interpreter's Bible*, vol. 1 (Nashville: Abingdon, 1994), 346.

94. Gen 2:9.

95. Gen 2:16.

96. Sarna, *Genesis*, 13.

97. Rev 19:19–21.

98. Rev 21:1–4.

99. Fretheim, "Genesis," 356.

100. N. T. Wright, *Surprised by Hope* (New York: HarperOne, 2008), 102.

101. Ware, *God's Greater Glory*, 67.

102. Ibid., 68.

103. I am suspending the fact that the Calvinist reading of scripture had already rendered it unintelligible and untrustworthy to me.

104. Piper, *The Pleasures of God*, 58.

105. Ibid., 55.

106. Boyd, *Is God to Blame?*, 178.

107. Phil 2:5–8.

108. Todd D. Still, *Philippians & Philemon*, Smyth and Helwys Bible Commentary (Macon, GA: Smith & Helwys, 2011), 68–69.

109. In the Lord's Prayer (Matt 6:10), Jesus teaches that God's will is not being done on earth as it is in heaven—hence the need to pray for it.

110. Moltmann, *The Crucified God*, 223.

111. Olson, *Against Calvinism*, 100.

112. Lewis, *Mere Christianity*, 41–42.

113. Jerry Walls, "The Free Will Defense, Calvinism, Wesley, and the Goodness of God," *Christian Scholar's Review* 13, no. 1 (1983), 25.

114. James Montgomery Boice, *Whatever Happened to the Gospel of Grace?* (Wheaton, IL.: Crossway, 2001), 167.

115. Ibid.

116. This is called prevenient grace. It is understood to be the powerful but resistible drawing of God in which one's fallen will is freed and given the chance to accept or reject God.

117. Olson, *Arminian Theology*, 159.

118. Indeed in Calvinism it is hard to understand why, if God hates human boasting so much, he has ordained so much of it and has ordained that this boasting will bring him glory.

119. Willard, *The Divine Conspiracy*, 38.

120. Alvin Plantinga, *God, Freedom, and Evil* (Grand Rapids; Eerdmans, 1977), 30.

121. In open theism, God does not know exactly which humans will end up in hell, but he must have a good idea that many humans will indeed be there, so I find the dilemma to be the same.

122. Just google "duck rabbit."

123. I owe this insight to Roger Olson and he fleshes this idea out in *Arminian Theology*, 72–73.

124. Ibid., 72.

125. George C. Berthold, "The Cappadocian Roots of Maximus the Confessor," in eds. F. Heinzer and C. von Schonborn, *Maximus Confessor, Actes du Symposium sure Maxime le Confesseur* (Fribourg: Editions Universitaires, 1982), 56.

126. Gen 31:3.

127. Frederick Buechner, *The Magnificent Defeat* (New York: Seabury Press, 1966), 18. I am greatly indebted to Buechner's masterful telling of this story in my less masterful telling.

128. Gen 32:28 (NIV).

129. Gen 32:31.

130. Buechner coined the phrase, "The Magnificent Defeat," while Brueggemann has suggested the phrase, "The Crippling Victory."

131. Daniel Taylor, *The Myth of Certainty* (Downers Grove, IL: InterVarsity), 79.

132. And famously, the only thing he found he could not doubt was his doubt. Or to put it another way, the only thing he was "certain" about was his existence as a doubting subject.

133. Newbigin, *Proper Confidence*, 27.

134. Or a completely unified community of persons to be exact—or to be inexact.

135. To spare you the quip—am I certain about this? Of course not, and that's the point!

136. Newbigin, *Proper Confidence*, 45.

137. Ibid., 61–62.

138. Ibid., 67.

139. Taylor, *The Myth of Certainty*, 94.

140. Buechner, *Wishful Thinking*, 23.

141. Karl Barth, *The Word of God and the Word of Man* (New York: Harper & Brothers, 1957), 186.

142. Wright, *How God Became King*, 6.

143. See Scot McKnight's *The King Jesus Gospel: The Original Good News Revisited* (Grand Rapids: Zondervan, 2011), N. T. Wright's *How God Became King*, and Dallas Willard's *The Divine Conspiracy* if you want some concise and stimulating insights into this topic.

144. Wright, *How God Became King*, 37.

145. McKnight, *The King Jesus Gospel*, 36.

146. For an excellent sketch of the gospel see ibid., 148–53.

147. Matt 4:17.

148. My translation of Mark 10:35–45.

149. Wright, *How God Became King*, 227.

150. Ibid., 239–40.

151. Dallas Willard, *The Spirit of the Disciplines: Understanding How God Changes Lives* (New York: HarperCollins, 1988), 258.

152. This is a painfully inadequate description of discipleship so *please* read *The Divine Conspiracy* by Dallas Willard.

153. Willard, *The Divine Conspiracy*, 301.

154. N. T. Wright, *Justification: God's Plan and Paul's Vision* (Downer's Grove, IL: InterVarsity, 2009), 37.

155. Ben Witherington III and Darlene Hyatt, *Paul's Letter to the Romans: A Socio-Rhetorical Commentary* (Grand Rapids: Eerdmans, 2004), 279.

156. Ibid., 249.

157. An insight I owe to N. T. Wright, "Romans," *The New Interpreter's Bible*, vol. 10 (Nashville: Abingdon, 1994), 622.

158. Paul Achtemeir, *Romans*, Interpretation (Atlanta: John Knox, 1985), 164–65.

159. Witherington and Hyatt, *Paul's Letter to the Romans*, 276–77.

Lightning Source UK Ltd.
Milton Keynes UK
UKOW01f0043180716

278533UK00003B/35/P